COMMUNITY IS THE WAY

ENGAGED WRITING AND DESIGNING
FOR TRANSFORMATIVE CHANGE

PRACTICES & POSSIBILITIES

Series Editors: Aimee McClure, Mike Palmquist, and Aleashia Walton

Series Associate Editor: Jagadish Paudel

The Practices & Possibilities Series addresses the full range of practices within the field of Writing Studies, including teaching, learning, research, and theory. From Joseph Williams' reflections on problems to Richard E. Young's taxonomy of "small genres" to Adam Mackie's considerations of technology, the books in this series explore issues and ideas of interest to writers, teachers, researchers, and theorists who share an interest in improving existing practices and exploring new possibilities. The series includes both original and republished books. Works in the series are organized topically.

The WAC Clearinghouse and University Press of Colorado are collaborating so that these books will be widely available through free digital distribution and low-cost print editions. The publishers and the series editors are committed to the principle that knowledge should freely circulate and have embraced the use of technology to support open access to scholarly work.

OTHER BOOKS IN THE SERIES

Jennifer Clary-Lemon, Derek Mueller, and Kate Pantelides, *Try This: Research Methods for Writers* (2022)

Jessie Borgman and Casey McArdle (Eds.), *Pars in Practice: More Resources and Strategies for Online Writing Instructors* (2021)

Mary Ann Dellinger and D. Alexis Hart (Eds.), *ePortfolios@edu: What We Know, What We Don't Know, And Everything In-Between* (2020)

Jo-Anne Kerr and Ann N. Amicucci (Eds.), *Stories from First-Year Composition: Pedagogies that Foster Student Agency and Writing Identity* (2020)

Patricia Freitag Ericsson, *Sexual Harassment and Cultural Change in Writing Studies* (2020)

Ryan J. Dippre, *Talk, Tools, and Texts: A Logic-in-Use for Studying Lifespan Literate Action Development* (2019)

Jessie Borgman and Casey McArdle, *Personal, Accessible, Responsive, Strategic: Resources and Strategies for Online Writing Instructors* (2019)

Cheryl Geisler and Jason Swarts, Coding *Streams of Language: Techniques for the Systematic Coding of Text, Talk, and Other Verbal Data* (2019)

Ellen C. Carillo, *A Guide to Mindful Reading* (2017)

Lillian Craton, Renée Love & Sean Barnette (Eds.), *Writing Pathways to Student Success* (2017)

Charles Bazerman, *Involved: Writing for College, Writing for Your Self* (2015)

COMMUNITY IS THE WAY

ENGAGED WRITING AND DESIGNING
FOR TRANSFORMATIVE CHANGE

By Aimée Knight

The WAC Clearinghouse
wac.colostate.edu
Fort Collins, Colorado

University Press of Colorado
upcolorado.com
Louisville, Colorado

The WAC Clearinghouse, Fort Collins, Colorado 80523

University Press of Colorado, Louisville, Colorado 80027

ISBN 978-1-64215-148-0 (PDF) | 978-1-64215-149-7 (ePub) | 978-1-64642-314-9 (pbk.)

DOI 10.37514/PRA-B.2022.1480

Produced in the United States of America

Library of Congress Cataloging-in-Publication Data

Names: Knight, Aimée, 1974– author.
Title: Community is the way : engaged writing and designing for transformative change / by Aimée Knight.
Description: Fort Collins, Colorado : The WAC Clearinghouse ; Louisville, Colorado : University Press of Colorado, [2022] | Series: Practices & possibilities | Includes bibliographical references and index.
Identifiers: LCCN 2022011158 (print) | LCCN 2022011159 (ebook) | ISBN 9781646423149 (paperback) | ISBN 9781642151480 (adobe pdf) | ISBN 9781642151497 (epub)
Subjects: LCSH: English language—Rhetoric—Study and teaching (Higher)—Social aspects—United States. | Transformative learning—United States. | Social justice and education—United States. | Community and college—United States.
Classification: LCC PE1404 .K576 2022 (print) | LCC PE1404 (ebook) | DDC 808/.0420711—dc23/eng/20220408
LC record available at https://lccn.loc.gov/2022011158
LC ebook record available at https://lccn.loc.gov/2022011159

Copyeditor: Karen P. Peirce
Designer: Mike Palmquist
Cover and Interior Photos: Aimée Knight
Series Editors: Aimee McClure, Mike Palmquist, and Aleashia Walton
Series Associate Editor: Jagadish Paudel

The WAC Clearinghouse supports teachers of writing across the disciplines. Hosted by Colorado State University, it brings together scholarly journals and book series as well as resources for teachers who use writing in their courses. This book is available in digital formats for free download at wac.colostate.edu.

Founded in 1965, the University Press of Colorado is a nonprofit cooperative publishing enterprise supported, in part, by Adams State University, Colorado State University, Fort Lewis College, Metropolitan State University of Denver, University of Alaska Fairbanks, University of Colorado, University of Denver, University of Northern Colorado, University of Wyoming, Utah State University, and Western Colorado University. For more information, visit upcolorado.com.

Land Acknowledgment. The Colorado State University Land Acknowledgment can be found at https://landacknowledgment.colostate.edu.

This book is for everyone who asks, *"How are we building community?"* and then takes the time to listen to the answer.

Contents

Acknowledgments

I wish to express my gratitude to the many community partners who shared their wisdom, knowledge, skills, and stories over the years. None of this work would be possible without them. A huge thanks to my students who put so much of themselves into their community-university partnerships—especially those that come back a second or even third time. Much gratitude to the editorial team, Mike Palmquist, Aimee Taylor, and Aleashia Walton, for their alchemical work guiding this manuscript. Karen Peirce, too, must be recognized as a master of her craft. Heartfelt thanks to Paula Mathieu for her thoughtful scholarship and enormous heart. A sincere thank you goes to my colleagues at Saint Joseph's University who feel more like family than coworkers. A special thank you to Tim Lockridge, who always seems to have the answers. I'm also indebted to Dànielle DeVoss, Jeff Grabill, Ellen Cushman, and Colleen Tremonte for their mentorship during my Ph.D. program in rhetoric and writing and for steering me toward the work that I love. A special thank you to my parents, both educators, for their inspiration and sage advice. To my friends and family—thank you for your encouragement throughout the many years of program building and book writing. Deepest gratitude to my husband, Chris, for his faith in me and everything I set my mind to. Any typos are attributed to my cats Islay and Harris.

Foreword. What Do We Want from Community Writing?

Paula Mathieu
BOSTON COLLEGE

I write this foreword at a moment when the climate in which we live is especially heated, both literally and figuratively. The planet warms and climate disasters increase while global action remains timid and piecemeal; U.S. neighborhoods remain segregated by race and income, which means so do our schools; borders and national boundaries breed tension and increased stigma and punishment of immigrants and refugees. Rifts widen between left and right politically, between those who value democracy and those who prefer order at any cost, between those who rely on science and vaccines and those who harbor distrust and fear, between those who see masks as a way for caring for self and others and those who equate masks with weakness and diminished freedom. Further heated rifts widen over issues like reproductive health, sexual assault, gender identity, sexual orientation, rights of people with disabilities, religion, ethnic identities, language policies. The list goes on and on. Underneath and fueling this rancor rests a bedrock of deep systemic inequality that for generations has tipped the scales in favor of those who are white and wealthy while punishing and harming bodies that are indigenous, black, and brown.

Can community writing help make this divided world a kinder, less oppressive place?

Positive social change is undoubtedly the *intention* of most if not all community-writing projects. At its heart, community writing projects accept that the world is imperfect, damaged, off-kilter, and at the same time seek to *do something* that brings a little change, a bit of positivity into a wounded world.

I was drawn to the work of community writing more than two decades ago because of its mix of utopian ambition and pragmatic project orientation. I longed to foster writing that acted as an agent in the world that strived to make it a little bit better. In *Tactics of Hope* (2005), I chronicled several community projects that provided income, a sense of community, and a public platform for adults and children experiencing homelessness, projects that gave writers support and audiences to tell stories and advocate for themselves and others. I argued that community-based work, then typically described as *service learning*, suffered a mismatch between the theories guiding it, which touted the value of reciprocity and collaboration, and many practices that focused more on the university's needs and student learning outcomes while paying less careful attention to the needs, values, and experiences of community partners.

In the past decade, much has changed to help make community writing projects even more ethical and accountable, including the Conference on College Composition and Communication (CCCC) issuing and revising the CCCC Statement on Community-Engaged Projects in Rhetoric and Composition[1] that outlines best practices in community-engaged work. The Coalition for Community Writing[2] (CCW) formed in 2015, has hosted three well-attended conferences, drawing a diverse group of scholars and community members from far and wide, and sponsors an annual award for outstanding community projects that helps to highlight innovative and equitably focused community projects. It also offers mentoring and support to all involved in community work, with a special focus on BIPOC emerging scholars.

Despite this necessary and valuable progress, community writing—as all writing—still suffers from inevitable blind spots that limit the value of this work or cause it to run counter to its intended aims. In *Mindful of Race: Transforming Racism for the Inside Out*, international teacher of meditation Ruth King describes the way that limited vision affects all people:

Common to all of us is the fact that we don't see the world as it is but how we have been conditioned to see it. The delusion we carry is that everyone sees—or should see—the world as we do. What we see or don't see has consequences. In general, white people do not see race unless they feel threatened or until someone brings it to their attention (2005, p. 65).

While everyone shares a partial and imperfect view of the world, the structures of power and privilege unequally fall to those who are white, who have money, are able-bodied, cis-gendered, heterosexual, young, and male. While the structures of inequality are multiple, one's ability to see and discuss race and whiteness, and King points out, is especially harmful and below the surface of one's day-to-day knowledge. White people (and I identify as white) can easily avoid issues of race, racism, and white supremacy, because the power and privileges we are afforded are often below the level of conscious noticing. White supremacy is our very culture—like fish in a pond, where are swimming in it, and can be barely aware of it.

Asao Inoue at his CCCC's 2019 Chair's address spoke directly about the deep ways that white supremacy structures our field and limits what is possible based on the bodies we inhabit. After first specifically addressing his "colleagues of color," he turned to specifically speak to the white majority in the audience: "I'm not going to say that you—you White folks in this room—are the special ones. You thinking you're special is the problem. It always has been, because you, and White people just like you who came before you, have had most of the power, decided most of the things, built the steel cage of White language supremacy that we exist in today, both in and outside of the academy—and likely, many of you didn't know you did it." Inoue argues that assumptions of white supremacy

1.   https://cccc.ncte.org/cccc/resources/positions/community-engaged
2.   https://communitywriting.org/

underscore what we uncritically adopt as commonsense and good writing. His words immediately and afterward caused discomfort and push back by some white scholars who felt singled out. While I sat with this critique and found it necessary for me to think deeply about what I assume or take for granted, I saw Inoue's talk as a gift, a necessary wake-up call from a friend and ally. I especially held to the following words:

> Just as it is unfair that in our world most indigenous, Latinx, and Black Americans will never get the chance to do what we do, to be teachers, or professors, or researchers, or something else that taps their own potentials because of the racist steel bars set around them, it is equally unfair that you [White scholars and teachers] perpetuate racism and White language supremacy not just through your words and actions, but through your body in a place like this or in your classrooms, despite your better intentions. Let me repeat that to compassionately urge you to sit in some discomfort: White people can perpetuate White supremacy by being present. You can perpetuate White language supremacy through the presence of your bodies in places like this.

Hurt and harm happen, no matter how good the intentions are. We remember that our intentions do not always mirror our impact. Students and community members with a history of racial trauma might see me, my white body, as threatening or traumatizing. That is a truth I need to sit with and deeply consider: how can community projects minimize harm and offer more than feel-good gestures? How can community writing address the systems of inequality and not merely bolster the status quo?

No single book can hope to address the harms of a culture built on systems of oppression. Any book that makes such grand claims should be suspect. But Aimée Knight's *Community is the Way: Engaged Writing and Design for Transformative Change* offers a method for working to engage in community writing more equitably by asking deep and important questions. First and foremost, this book does not see *community* as a noun, an entity that already exists, but instead frames community as an action, a goal. Partnerships *aim to build community*. It can happen, with a lot of care and work, but it's not a foregone conclusion. One must see the multiple audiences even within a single nonprofit and ask questions like Whose public? Whose idea of good? For whom? Who decides? "The public good" is contested and shifting, and work that enters that arena must be prepared to take sides.

Additionally innovative in Knight's work is deep and skilled engagement with the tools of social networking, web platforms, and public storytelling. This is the work that all advocacy organizations need but often lack the capacity to do well. It's a space where writing and digital literacy skills can help achieve the project that a created community defines.

To seek to forge and create community requires both intellectual and internal work. Knight outlines the steps for what she calls *equity-based approaches* in community writing: an inquiry that prioritizes the need of the community, building empathy, co-creating knowledge, researching, composing and recomposing, testing and revision, and evaluating capacity. These are important and useful ideas, a North Star, as she calls it, values that serve less as goals but more as questions that prompt us "to do better work with our partners to build more just and transformative worlds." I like this structure because it frames all work as questing and imperfect. It's not a question of *if* we make mistakes but *when* and *what will we do in response when we make them*?

The gaps between intention and impact, what we think we're doing and what we are actually doing, especially when the "we" are people with more racial, economic, and cultural capital than the community members with whom we work are deep, complex, and not easy to reconcile. Rather than seeking to eliminate or ignore them, I believe we need to sit with and become curious and open to facing these gaps, the failures, the ways we fall short, if we are going to do work that does more than uphold the status quo. Inoue encourages "sitting with" our discomfort, engaging mindfully and intentionally with the ways that white supremacy structures the world we inhabit. "Because racism is so intricately woven into our social fabric, it is difficult to both discern and discuss. Yet, fundamental to understanding our habits of harm is understanding and contemplating the stained soil of racism and racial trauma in US history" (King, 2018, p. 43).

Understanding and contemplating. Two of the tools that Ruth King offers as necessary for starting to create empathy and the kind of community that this book hopes to build: both intellectual mind and embodied awareness. We need to engage intellectually to understand our own privileges and the blind spots that our situatedness encourages. But we also need a deep and ongoing contemplative practice that helps us build the embodied capacity to sit with discomfort, an ability to learn poise, readiness, to act without reactivity, at least that's where my current writing keeps leading me again and again. Contemplative work can help us build the emotional resilience necessary to allow us to enter spaces bravely and calmly; to become curious and open to difference and changing our minds; to communicate directly with honesty, respect, and compassion; to speak up when we feel hurt and listen with an open spirit when we cause hurt; to listen, stay curious, seeking facts, ideas, and new possibilities; to invite healing through forgiveness and making amends. And most of all, we acknowledge that when we fail, we will try again.

Ultimately, there is no end goal to justice work. We are not called on to complete it, nor are we exempted from its responsibility. Layla Saad (2020) writes, "There is no feel-good reward at the end other than the knowledge that you are doing this because it's the right thing to do. . . . You won't get any ally cookies for it. You won't be celebrated for it. You will have to learn to wean yourself off the addiction to instant gratification and instead develop a consciousness for doing what is right even if nobody ever thanks you for it" (pp. 25–26). Jacqueline Jones Royster (2017) invokes the metaphor of a relay race as a way to view her role in the struggle for justice—she runs her leg as fully as she can and then passes the baton forward, trusting the work will go on. And while we continue running, may we be fueled by models and methods like Aimée Knight's, as we seek to unlearn, learn, grow, and organize toward equity.

References

Inoue, Asao. (2019, March 4). How do we languaging so people stop killing each other, or what do we do about white language supremacy? [Chair's address]. Conference on College Composition and Communication, Pittsburg, PA.

King, Ruth. (2018). *Mindful of race: Transforming racism from the inside out.* Sounds True.

Mathieu, Paula. (2005). *Tactics of hope: The public turn in english composition.* Heinemann.

Mathieu, Paula. (2014). Excavating indoor voices: Inner rhetoric and the mindful writing teacher" *Journal of Advanced Composition, 34*(1–2), 173–190.

Mathieu, Paula. (2016). Being there: Mindfulness as ethical classroom practice. *Journal for the Assembly of Expanded Perspectives on Learning, 21*(Winter), 14–20.

Mathieu, Paula. (2020). Mindful ethics and mindful writing. In John Duffy & Lois Agnew (Eds.), *After Plato: Rhetoric, ethics, and the teaching of writing* (pp. 212–228). Utah State University Press.

Royster, Jacqueline Jones. (2017, October 5). Coalitions, (r)evolutions, and celebrations [Lunchtime keynote]. Feminisms and Rhetoric Conference, Dayton, OH.

Saad, Layla. (2020). *me and white supremacy.* Sourcebooks.

COMMUNITY IS THE WAY

ENGAGED WRITING AND DESIGNING
FOR TRANSFORMATIVE CHANGE

Introduction. Lesson (Still Not) Learned

On an October day, while attending a workshop at the Conference on Community Writing, a well-known scholar made a racially biased comment during her slide presentation. *Did she just say that?* I felt the tension creeping toward my neck. Ironically, the presenter's talk focused on social justice pedagogies and how she engages in writing projects in her community. I can't say whether the presenter knew how the comment came across to workshop participants. But the longer I sat there, the more uncomfortable I became with the statement and what I felt was my responsibility to address it. While I tried to refocus my attention on the talk, the comment had done its work. Although it had not been openly hostile or even intentional, its words had a quieter effect. They made me perceive the presenter as sheltered, privileged, ensconced in the ivory tower, as someone with a touch of a savior complex—not the effect we are going for as scholars having a conversation about social justice and community writing. Regrettably, I didn't speak up. *Should I interrupt the talk to discuss what she said? Will I appear overly righteous? More than 20 minutes have passed; it's just too late.*

Another workshop participant—coincidentally, a former Writing Studies graduate student of mine and the only Black woman in the room—eventually did speak up. As we gathered around a table for a workshop activity, she gracefully brought up to the group the presenter's comment. It hung there above the table for a startling moment. Then the denials began. Unfortunately, the presenter did not stop to listen and consider what the workshop participant had to say. Instead, the presenter steadfastly "doubled down," with no acknowledgment of the potential harm done. This dismissal (and I'm guessing here) was likely an all-too-human defense mechanism to save face. No doubt, the participant's comment, however congenially delivered, didn't fit with the presenter's self-perceived identity—how she saw herself as a person in the world. The other co-presenters corralled around her—each dismissing any possibility of guilt or harm done. This is another related issue: we are not always aware of our blinders or our blunders. Even when someone tries to inform us collegially, we might not be able to hear it. I imagine that this issue is even more complicated if social justice and community engagement issues are a large part of our position as scholars. This tendency can be attributed, at least in part, to confirmation bias, "the tendency for people to embrace information that supports their beliefs and reject information that contradicts them" (Kolbert, 2017).

I've rehearsed how it could have gone differently. During the presentation, I could have found the courage to say, "I'm curious about the use of 'the comment,' can you tell us more about that?" That might have loosened up a generative conversation with the group. It could have invited people to share their insights and perspectives about who might be harmed by the comment or whose experience could have been minimized. It could have been an opening for them to share how the statement affected them and how to imagine other, more helpful ways to frame ideas or think about what language we might want to use in the future as a community of scholars and writing teachers. When confronted by the workshop participant, the presenter (or any of her co-presenters) could have deferred judgment in favor of understanding. They could have validated her experience. They could have listened with compassion. There could have been a productive conversation to invite not just a teaching moment but also a community-building moment for us as a field. It didn't happen, and I know that at least two of us, consequently, felt even more uncomfortable while gathered around the table. Ideally, the workshop participant shouldn't have had to speak up. While I am grateful that she did, she shouldn't have had to shoulder that work alone. This incident left her insulted twice over. For her, the conference room had become a hostile environment that protected whiteness. And I'm not sure the audience even noticed. This incident left me seriously wondering about the harm we might be doing regularly—without even being aware.

Asking "How am I doing harm?" or "How are we doing harm?" is tricky and humbling. It's a question we must address in our IRBs, in our evaluations, in our classrooms, and in working with communities. An honest reckoning with this question is more complex than I would like to admit, as I hope this story illustrates. This is a story that is happening everywhere, and it could have been almost any of us standing up there that day in front of the data projector. It probably has been us. I want to show, through this anecdote, how self-interested, insulated, and colonizing we in academia can be—even unwittingly. Despite touting current social justice pedagogies and anti-racist and decolonial methods, we may enact the very thing we are fighting against without even realizing it. I'm not recounting this story to induce guilt and self-reproach. I want us to be realistic about the fact that we are still living and working within oppressive systems. Nowhere is this awareness more critical than in working with community partners. Probably like you, I'm invested in social justice and working with historically underinvested communities. And possibly like you, I've carried my unintentional baggage and colonizing behaviors beyond the classroom walls and into the community—even while trying not to. This book is about working together toward designing more intentional, more equitable partnerships. It attempts to answer the question "What does it look like to center equity and social justice in our community writing work?"

Justice by Design

This book is about equity-based approaches to writing and designing with communities—methods that have grown from theory and practice within the field. Without a commitment to equity-based and decolonial approaches in our community-engaged writing partnerships, we risk the danger of contributing to the reproduction of systemic oppression. As the opening anecdote illustrates, it's all too easy to be unaware of the harm we might cause. It's all too easy to uphold the status quo and carry out the inequity designed into our systems and institutions—probably even into our own writing programs. If we haven't done the work to understand how to create more inclusive and equitable outcomes with community partners, we are inadvertently adhering to default settings, which include colonial mindsets, unconscious assumptions, and self-interested agendas. Without doing this work, we are complicit in a system designed to uphold injustice. After all, our systems reproduce what they are designed to produce. In the vein of disrupting this pattern, the Creative Reaction Lab in St. Louis, Missouri, was founded as a nonprofit community action organization focusing on civic leadership. The Creative Reaction Lab (2019) has contended that "systems of oppression, inequality, and inequity are by design; therefore, they can and *must* be redesigned. . . . We all have the power to influence outcomes. Every choice that we make every day contribute to a greater design" (para. 3). As this organization has suggested, intentionally centering equity and justice when collaborating with communities requires us to consciously redesign both mindsets and infrastructures to move us toward more just and equitable partnerships. The approaches shared in this book work toward that goal.

Although this is a book of many questions, one guides the entire work: Are we engaging in a process that builds community? When we center the community, and the community's vision, above everything else in the context of a research partnership, we change our approaches to community-engaged writing. When we hold our collaborations up to this question, we "have to adjust our lines of inquiry and our discourse to be sure we are engaging with communities with every effort to partner mutually with, and to the equal benefit of, our communities" (Bortolin, 2011, p. 56). By putting the community's gains first (over the university gains and commitments such as our publications, grants, and even student learning outcomes), we can frame our research as "a process which builds community," and our "research can be viewed as community-building" (Checkoway, 2015, p. 139). Community-building approaches pursue social justice. They are equity-focused approaches to collaborative partnerships that call on a community's resources and strengths. A community-building process entails

- a focus on assets versus a focus on needs;
- a focus on strengths versus a focus on issues;
- a focus on asset-mapping versus needs assessment;
- a focus on community as co-creators versus beneficiaries;
- a focus on strategies versus a focus on problem-solving;
- a focus on community knowledge versus expert knowledge;
- a focus on amplifying voices versus giving voice to the voiceless;
- a focus on internal agency and capacity-building versus outside "saviors";
- a focus on a solid and capable community versus a poor, struggling community;

- a focus on creating collaborative relationships versus transactional relationships; and
- a focus on the community members as producers versus community members as needy people seeking services.

When we shift the focus to putting the community first and viewing our partnerships as community-building enterprises, we can better commit to creating conditions for reciprocity and mutuality with our partners. Community writing scholars, working toward more equitable partnerships for decades, are uniquely positioned to lead the way in designing more just and ethical collaborations with community partners. As examined in Chapter 1, community writing scholars have led important ethical conversations around reciprocal partnerships, infrastructure, and the public good—longtime discussions in the field. However, there is a point where those conversations are failing us. As Paula Mathieu (2005) noted in *Tactics of Hope: The Public Turn in English Composition,* "Our scholarship does a good job of spelling out tenets and guidelines for street work. The difficulty lies in how to move from calls for reciprocity, public action, and self-reflexivity toward specific ways of acting and imagining concrete visions in local times and places" (p. 20). Although numerous theories of co-creation, mutuality, and reciprocity circulate in the field's literature, community-based writing practitioners may still find it hard to put such theories into practice. Katrina M. Powell and Pamela Takayoshi (2003) argued that theorizing about the complex ethical issues practitioners can find themselves in and actually doing the work can be two different things, warning, "Without narratives of prior experiences that suggest some of the ethical terrain, researchers can find themselves unprepared for responding to dilemmas that arise in the processes of researching. . . . As a field, we have very few guidelines for ethical, appropriate decision making 'in the moment'" (p. 401). Robbin D. Crabtree (2008) suggested that "we need more than an ethos of reciprocity as a guide; we need to learn the theories, methods, and on-the-ground strategies that are more likely to produce mutuality in process and outcomes" (p. 26). Jessica Shumake and Rachael W. Shah (2017) also acknowledged the large number of theories and calls for reciprocity but lamented that "these theories may remain anemic because they are not grounded in practices that grow organically from doing community-based work" (p. 11).

The field of community writing values the co-creation of knowledge and strives for more generative forms of collaboration with our partners. Part of this work involves deepening our forms of evidence and our stories of actual, on-the-ground reciprocity. Another part of this work involves building applicable methods to design community writing partnerships that can reflect these richer forms of engagement. As our scholarship acknowledges, there are many articles and books that sustain theories, evaluation, and critique; fewer resources make visible the everyday, local action that we implement in our classrooms and in our communities. The hands-on tactics in this book are offered in the spirit of filling that implementation gap and providing a specific vision of how to enact social justice work with community partners. Throughout the book, readers will find much-needed examples of concrete, situated action that have grown organically out of disciplinary knowledge and fieldwork running a community writing program in Philadelphia that has sustained well over 100 partnerships. This book argues for a community-building approach to writing partnerships that centers justice and equity in our work. This work demands that we commit to a process that leads us to consider how power, oppression, resistance, privilege, penalties, benefits, and harms are systematically designed into the very systems we want to change. By asking, "How are we building community?" in each step of the research process, we better commit to creating conditions for reciprocity and mutuality with our partners and supporting their visions for transformational change.

Chapter Overview

This book is for writing teachers seeking to enact socially just, civically engaged collaborations with community partners. The primary audience for this book is teachers of community writing and those in writing studies, computers and writing, service-learning, digital humanities, and technical communication who engage in community partnerships that pursue social justice. Natasha N. Jones (2020) has argued for moving toward coalitional learning—what disciplines can learn from each other—"especially in regard to how each discipline engages with issues of social justice" (p. 517). Rebecca W. Walton and co-authors (2019) proposed, in *Technical Communication After the Social Justice Turn: Building Coalitions for Action,* that all members of the field of writing studies invest in social justice through a coalitional framework, but they noted the "field has yet to establish what that work can or should look like" (p. 5). In an attempt to address this gap, this book demonstrates how to co-create class projects with community partners (local not-for-profit and community-based organizations) from an equity-based, community-building perspective. Whether it ultimately sparks a conversation, a media assignment, a method for collaboration, or even a vision for a future writing program, I hope this book offers something of value for those seeking more intentional and socially just approaches to writing and designing with communities. The approaches offered here are examples of how we might draw on our disciplinary knowledge and experience to create equity-based approaches to writing and designing with communities. These include

- Chapter 1—ways to enact mutual and reciprocal partnerships;
- Chapter 2—ways to conduct design research with communities;
- Chapter 3—ways to engage in community-building approaches in a writing classroom;
- Chapter 4—ways to approach media and social change in the classroom for capacity-building; and

- Chapter 5—ways to become a better ally to communities via student learning, infrastructure, and decolonial methods.

How might we enact a transforming commitment to social justice by engaging in projects that benefit the community and the university? Chapter 1 begins by exploring the broader call for mutual and reciprocal partnerships in the context of community-engaged scholarship. Universities are increasingly placing a high value on opportunities to translate academic knowledge into collaborative projects that benefit both the community and university. Community-engaged scholar Derek Barker (2004) asserted that "the language of engagement suggests an element of reciprocal and collaborative knowledge production that is unique to these forms of scholarship" (p. 126). In community-engaged scholarship, not only do we deepen what it means to be civically involved, but we also learn more about what it means to collaborate "with communities in the production of knowledge" (Barker, 2004, p. 126). Part of our work moving forward is how to orient our partnerships so that both community-based knowledge and university-based knowledge are valued in a true "context of partnership and reciprocity" (Commission on Public Purpose in Higher Education, n.d., Defining Community Engagement section). Writing studies scholarship looking at the nature of community-university partnerships has much to offer the community engagement movement. Guiding principles gleaned from the field's literature represent signposts emerging from within writing studies. These principles can provide a framework for our own goals and aims as we work with communities.

How might we join in a process of inquiry with community partners that embodies the values of mutuality and reciprocity? Chapter 2 focuses on methods of networked collaboration in community-engaged partnerships. Four approaches to collaboration are examined: (a) design thinking, (b) co-design, (c) design justice, and (d) equity-based approaches to community writing. Brief definitions of each of these approaches are as follows:

- *Design thinking* is an audience-centered approach to creative problem solving. The design thinking process features a method of inquiry that favors empathizing, bias to action, and the prototyping and testing of solutions. This approach favors a client-designer relationship.

- *Co-design* is a collaborative approach with roots in participatory design techniques. A fundamental tenet of co-design is the building and deepening of equal collaboration between citizens affected by or attempting to resolve a particular design challenge. Co-design positions participants as experts of their own experience, thus becoming central to the design process.

- *Design justice* is an approach that focuses explicitly on "how design reproduces and challenges the matrix of domination (white supremacy, heteropatriarchy, capitalism, ableism, settler colonialism, and other forms of structural inequality)" (Costanza-Chock, 2020, Introduction section). Design justice is also a growing community of practice that ensures a more equitable distribution of design's benefits and burdens, meaningful participation in design decisions, and recognition of community-based, Indigenous, and diasporic design traditions, knowledge, and practices.

- *Equity-based approaches* in community writing emerge organically from theory and practice in the field. Focusing on community building requires us to intentionally redesign both mindsets and infrastructures to share power and decision making with our partners. Equity-based approaches include building empathy, framing inquiry, co-creating knowledge, researching, composing and recomposing, testing and revision, and evaluating capacity. This flexible approach for conducting design research with communities can point us toward more just and equitable partnerships.

A discussion of the challenges and affordances of each method as well as a discussion of which method would work best in a given writing classroom situation is included.

How might we engage in the classroom in community-building approaches that pursue social justice via emerging media? Chapter 3 examines how we can employ emerging media to both build up and engage powerfully with communities, allies, stakeholders, and policymakers. When community partners build capacity with emerging media platforms and literacies, they can make an impact, even with modest resources—becoming more effective in their work and their reach as they challenge injustices and systemic inequalities. Engaging in media projects with community partners helps organizations grow, making them even more effective at creating change in our communities. Emerging media projects provide our community partners with the tools and strategies they need to create a more effective, lasting change. This chapter features the Beautiful Social Research Collaborative, a community engaged writing program I founded in 2010 at Saint Joseph's University in Philadelphia, Pennsylvania. The collaborative employs three approaches to working with community partners on course projects that pursue social justice via emerging media: (a) media projects, (b) training projects, and (c) research projects. The collaborative is committed to working with community organizations to carry out projects with real-world impact that advance and share knowledge about media and communication. Students in this writing program have led free of charge more than one hundred projects with communities. These projects have involved new media and social web consultancy, training, professional writing, social media management, online survey design, web design, and web-based video. The driving aim behind this collaborative is not just to achieve measurable impact or results on any given project (rewarding in its own right) but rather to create mutually beneficial relationships with allies who are committed to building just and equitable futures. This chapter concludes with a case study of our work with our community partner Life

After Life, illustrating our equity-based approach to writing and designing with communities. This section provides an inside view of the situated local action and decision-making process that guides the Beautiful Social Research Collaborative's work but that is often invisible from view.

How might we develop our students' skills in writing and rhetoric via emerging media while working with our community partners to build capacity? Chapter 4 offers writing teachers a series of practical media analysis projects that build capacity for community partners. Through media analysis, students learn to strategically leverage media platforms to advocate with and for community organizations. Students learn to frame themselves as participants within a learning community through these activities as they examine and participate in timely issues and tools pertinent to work in professional and technical writing, digital rhetoric, new media, advocacy, nonprofit communications, and organizational storytelling. Students conduct a series of activities, each addressed in separate sections of the chapter and briefly described as follows:

- **Design question analysis**—This analysis activity frames inquiry around a community-identified goal and works to structure the project. A design question is a clear statement about a phenomenon of interest, a condition to be improved upon, an opportunity to be explored, or a question that exists in theory or practice for the partner's field or organization. Since our partnerships are based on a community-driven desire to build capacity or to create change, this question should originate from the community partner. We then work with partners to refine the query.
- **Social media analysis**—In this analysis, groups observe and describe the state of the community partner's social media platforms. This activity examines our partner's platform tactics, content, and audience interactions. This analysis aims to arrive at a clear awareness of how our community partners are currently using social media platforms and to identify opportunities for future action.
- **Comparative media analysis**—In this activity, groups compare media drawn from three mentor accounts. Based on the section "Nonprofit Examples of Excellence" in *Social Media for Social Good: A How-To Guide for Nonprofits* by Heather Mansfield (2011), students construct their comparisons tailored to the organization's needs. By locating three mentor accounts, groups explore potential strategies and possibilities for our community partners to employ.
- **Golden circle analysis**—Sometimes called "knowing your why," the golden circle is an effective tactic to get a bird's eye view of an organization (Sinek, 2011, p. 50). The golden circle helps map an organization's why, how, and what and was popularized in brand strategist Simon Sinek's 2011 book *Start With Why: How Great Leaders Inspire Everyone to Take Action*, which examines how inspiring leaders communicate.

- **Social object rhetorical analysis**—Drawing from contemporary social theorists Karin Knorr Cetina (1997, 2001, 2007) and Jyri Engeström (2005), we look at how people connect through shared objects. The argument here is that the object is the thing that links people together. Understanding social objects can help bridge an essential gap between (a) the more formal and technical aspects of design and (b) the social and cultural aspects of how social objects engage users and build communities.

- **Organizational storytelling**—A story for a nonprofit is a way for an organization (a nonhuman entity) to *humanize* itself. By leading with a heartfelt story, our partners can elicit a strong sense of *pathos* while engaging deeply with their audience on a personal level. This section examines storytelling mechanisms, including a "story generator" that can be used to create various content—from long-form articles, to blog posts, to social media campaigns, to takeovers, to lone social media posts.

After students conduct these activities, they can be combined into a community partner report. This substantive report offers our partners custom approaches to engaging their audience via emerging media.

How do community writing partnerships influence the concept of *agency*— ideas about the ability to act in and on the world in ways that relate to civic purposes? When collaborating with organizations, students learn how to take writing and emerging media beyond the personal and entertainment and into places for activism and social change. Chapter 5 delves into some of the affordances of attempting this kind of work in the writing classroom and discusses my preliminary research findings on agency and how community partnerships influence students' ideas about design, community, power, and beliefs. These findings support writing instructors as they move concerns beyond classroom walls and consider pedagogies that feature collaborations that are wired for meaningful experience, activism, and community engagement.

To become a vital resource to communities outside university walls, we need to view our community-engaged teaching and research as a form of community building. The book concludes by examining the changes that can occur to center community building in our work, particularly our approaches to equity, our investment in intentional infrastructure, and our commitment to decolonial methods. When designing equity-based approaches, not only do we need to consider how to share power and knowledge with our partners, we need to support the building of internal capacity from within our local communities. Writing partnerships can leverage community-building approaches to support local grassroots activism, decolonization efforts, co-resistance movements, and social change initiatives. By centering equity and solidarity in our work, design can be "an ethical praxis of world making" (Escobar, 2018, p. 313).

Chapter 1. How Might We Enact a Transforming Commitment to Social Justice by Engaging in Projects That Benefit Both the Community and the University?

This book examines how our work in the writing classroom can enact social justice and shape social change through equity-based collaborative partnerships with local organizations. Community-engaged writing takes place on many college campuses in both formal and grassroots initiatives. This chapter addresses writing projects and programs seeking to employ community-building approaches to create more equitable partnerships.

The Terms of Community-Engaged Scholarship

Universities are increasingly placing a high value on translating academic resources into collaborative initiatives that benefit both the community and the university. Through collaborative partnerships, both faculty and students participate in community-engaged scholarship. This movement became popular in the 1990s when Ernest L. Boyer (1996), former Carnegie Foundation president, claimed that "the academy must become a more vigorous partner in the search for answers to our most pressing social, civic, economic, and moral problems, and must reaffirm its historic commitment to . . . the scholarship of engagement" (p. 11). Put plainly, community-engaged scholarship today "reflects a growing interest in broadening and deepening the public aspects of academic scholarship" (Barker, 2004, p. 123). As engagement scholar Drew Pearl (2020) acknowledged, "In the world of community engagement, we understand that the word "scholarship" refers to much more than our research" (p. 1). Engaged scholarship, or community-engaged scholarship, is research that puts the university's academic resources to work in contributing to the public good. It consists of (a) research, teaching, integration, and application scholarship that (b) incorporates reciprocal practices of civic engagement into the production of knowledge (Barker, 2004, p. 124). Barker (2004) asserted that "the language of engagement suggests an element of reciprocal and collaborative knowledge production that is unique to these forms of scholarship" (126). In community-engaged projects, not only can we deepen our understanding of what it means to be civically engaged, but we also learn more about what it means to collaborate "with communities in the production of knowledge" (Barker, 2004, p. 126).

In 2021, over 360 U.S. colleges and universities have received the Carnegie Community Engagement Classification, an elective designation that indicates an institutional commitment to community engagement by the Carnegie Foundation for the Advancement of Teaching. The foundation defines community engagement as "collaboration between institutions of higher education and their larger communities (local, regional, state, national, global) for the mutually beneficial exchange of knowledge and resources in a context of partnership and reciprocity" (Driscoll, 2008, p. 39). Additionally, Campus Compact (n.d.-c) is "a national coalition of colleges and universities . . . dedicated . . . to campus-based civic engagement . . . to develop students' citizenship skills and forge effective community partnerships" (Campus Compact Overview).

Mutuality and Reciprocity

Community-university partnerships offer higher education institutions and the communities in which they are located enormous potential for mutual benefit. Generally, a community-university collaboration is lauded as a joint "win/win" by both parties. Universities have a stake in improving their communities' local economy, health, and culture on a fundamental level. The university benefits from partnerships by advancing academic engagement—working toward original contributions to disciplinary questions while engaging with communities—and working directly with community members or with organizations that work on behalf of those communities, such as nonprofit organizations. Studies show that faculty members who engage in community engagement have more publications in peer-reviewed journals, more funded research projects, and higher student evaluations of their teaching than those who do not (Doberneck et al., 2010). Not only are partnerships generative for relevant scholarship, research, and creative activity, but also, they enrich teaching and learning in order to prepare educated engaged citizens, strengthen democratic values and civic responsibility, address critical societal issues, and contribute to the public good (Fitzgerald et al., 2005).

The community benefits from university partnerships as well, with the stated end goal generally being to work together toward creating new knowledge or building capacity. This could take the shape of something as concrete as a new resource or deliverable, or something more abstract such as an improved method or approach to operations. In most cases, the community partner gains from the collaboration new knowledge, resources, or capacity it ordinarily would not have. University programs can partner with local groups and organizations, schools, and nonprofits. Through this work, organizations grow in skills and capacity while fulfilling their missions, making them more effective at shaping lasting change.

The Carnegie Community Engagement classification is the leading framework for institutionalizing community engagement in U.S. higher education, currently taking place every two years and requiring evidence-based documentation of institutional practice to be used in the process of self-assessment and quality improvement. Universities may seek classification for community engagement to support the university mission and encourage self-study on how the university connects with local, regional, and global communities. The classification process invites the university to identify current best practices, envision future opportunities for engagement, and earn public recognition for the university's commitment to contribute to the public good. (The Elective Classification for Community Engagement, 2022).

A recent national survey of 100 urban universities and colleges conducted through the University of Virginia's Institute for Advanced Studies focused on the current state of community-university partnerships. The resulting report indicated, "As the influence of the Carnegie Foundation's classification suggests, accrediting bodies have the unique ability to incentivize university leadership to prioritize community engagement as well as provide objective feedback and recommended next steps" (Yates & Accardi, 2019, p. 35). A growing number of colleges and universities are considering community engagement as a primary indicator in the granting of tenure and promotion, the conferring of grants and other awards, and the determination of merit raises, increasing both the value and visibility of community-engagement efforts at the institutional level.

While many of our institutions are riding the wave of community engagement (or, as the trend indicates, will soon be), the movement is not without its critiques. Despite the growing demand to pursue and promote community-university partnerships, they remain a challenging work in progress, in part because "many universities have a fraught history of failed, even parasitic, relationships with their local communities" (Yates & Accardi, 2019, p. 6). In addition to the problem of unethical partnerships, infrastructure and resources remain significant hurdles. Community-engaged initiatives and programs are frequently "sporadic, disconnected or redundant in nature, supported by individual faculty, specific funding or fleeting leadership, without incentives for broad-based support or long-term institutional commitment" (Yates & Accardi, 2019, p. 6).

With the growing demand for more community engagement at our universities (fueled in part by the sought-after Carnegie classification), the field of writing studies has informed meaningful, ethical conversations around reciprocal partnerships, infrastructure, and the public good—longtime discussions in the discipline. The field of community writing, working across borders and locales for decades, is uniquely positioned to help guide this growing movement in higher education.

A major strength of the field lies in its ability to extend, complicate, critique, and ultimately enrich notions of what it means to engage in the "mutually beneficial exchange of knowledge and resources in a context of partnership and reciprocity" (Commission on Public Purpose in Higher Education, n.d., Defining Community Engagement section)—a subject to which nearly every university has directed its gaze. Writing studies scholars looking at the nature of community-university partnerships pose relevant questions that are timely to the community engagement movement:

- "Are we privileging ourselves over the community?" (Bortolin, 2011, p. 55).
- "Where is the *community* in the literature?" (Cruz & Giles, 2000, p. 28).
- "Do they continue their lives unchanged? If not, how do they articulate the benefits?" (Ball & Goodburn, 2000, p. 82).
- "How can universities and communities collaborate in ways that are genuinely mutually beneficial?" (Yates & Accardi, 2019, p. 44).
- "What are the ethical obligations and responsibilities of community partnerships?" (Taufen, 2018, p. 7).
- "Engagement for what, to what end?" (Saltmarsh & Hartley, 2012, p. 9).

Guiding Principles

Three guiding principles emerge from scholarship on community writing partnerships. These principles represent signposts of thought emerging from the field of writing studies. They are presented here as an entryway to working with community partners. The principles are offered in the spirit of a conversation starter and as signals in a process rather than as an ending point or a perfect formula for community-engaged work. A centralized process for working with community partners would be the opposite of what this book is trying to achieve. Instead, inspired by the Allied Media Projects' (n.d.) network principles and the Design Justice Network's (n.d.) principles, the guiding principles offered here can be viewed as an inclusive set of values that guides various types of work in the fields of writing studies, community writing, computers and writing, and technical and professional communication. These principles can provide a starting framework for our goals and aims as we work with communities:

1. We prioritize the strengths and assets of our community partners. When working with community partners, we focus on the assets inherent in the community while building capacity for improvement.
2. We value the co-creation of new knowledge with our community partners. When working with community partners, we create reciprocal, generative spaces for the co-creation of knowledge.
3. We are committed to a process of transformative change. When working with community partners, the impact on the community is prioritized throughout the process.

Guiding Principle 1: We Prioritize the Strengths and Assets of Our Community Partners

How are we defining "community?" Is the project approached through a strengths-based view (rather than a deficit-based view)? The first guiding principle intentionally frames work with our partners as a relationship that focuses foremost on the partner—rather than the university. The nature of community-engaged work dictates that we direct our energy at real-world issues that are defined by communities "as we locate ourselves within the democratic process of everyday teaching and learning in our neighborhoods" (Cushman, 1996, p. 12). Although it may sound obvious, even self-evident at this point, there is much riding on this statement for the field of community writing. Prioritizing community partners orients our work in a way that puts our partner's gains first, rather than the gains of the university. Historically this has not always been the case. Nadinne I. Cruz and Dwight E. Giles (2000) identified several reasons for the lack of attention on communities in engagement scholarship. For one, they noted that since the 1990s, community-based learning has focused on validating the discipline itself, tending to academic concerns, faculty perceptions, and student learning outcomes. It is a relatively common occurrence in community-university partnerships that "university representatives frequently exercise more agency in partnerships, controlling money, setting schedules based on university timelines, privileging student over community outcomes, speaking with discourses and epistemologies tied to power, publishing about community members, and holding more institutional clout and resources" (Shumake & Shah, 2017. p. 12). Additionally, "funders, seeking to document and evaluate their investments, have made student outcome research a priority in their grant-making" instead of a research focus on community impact (Cruz & Giles, 2000, p. 28).

When putting community first, it is necessary to look at how we attend to and define "community." Many studies use the term "community" when referring exclusively to nonprofit participation (Vernon & Ward, 1999). Who or what is the community when we in the fields of writing studies and community writing refer to it? The community could be located in service-learning partners, nonprofit leadership members, ad hoc community groups, student groups, agencies, agencies' clients, a geographic location, or even a virtual network (to name a few). This first principle asks us to consider where we work, prioritizing the community in our research, which for some may start with defining what kind of community we are in partnership with. While it might (again) sound obvious, it is not always a cut-and-dried definition, and the waters can quickly get murky. For example, when considering a nonprofit organization as a community partner—is that organization "the community"? Can the nonprofit be accountable to speak on behalf of a community? What happens when the viewpoints of the broader community at large differ from the nonprofits that intend to serve them?

In a study of 85 qualitative interviews conducted in three low-income Philadelphia neighborhoods, researchers Rebecca J. Kissane and Jeff Gingerich (2004) compared how nonprofit directors (n = 51) and community residents (n = 34) perceived their neighborhoods' problems. They found that nonprofit leaders and community residents drifted apart in their assessments of the neighborhoods, holding widely disparate perspectives. For example, they noted that nonprofit leaders indicated lack of jobs and job training as significant problems in the area, while lack of youth services, followed by lack of food programs, were indicated as problems by community residents. The researchers found that not only do nonprofit leaders hold varying viewpoints from community residents but also possibly from the nonprofit organization's funders and donors. To be sure, this is a complex issue, warranting ongoing attention. However, what is telling is the degree to which we (and, here, I mean teachers in writing studies) might presume that the nonprofit organizations represent and serve the community, that the nonprofit organization is valuable to its community, and that the nonprofit organization is accountable to its community. We (and, here, I mean I) have often conflated the two, working under the assumption that partnering directly with a nonprofit is one of the best ways to benefit the community as a whole.

When working with communities, writing scholars recommend a focus on assets, referring to asset-based community development (Cruz & Giles, 2000; Diehl et al., 2008; Saltmarsh et al., 2009; Shah et al., 2018), a movement embraced by the community engagement field, "standing as a touchstone for respectful and effective ways of framing communities" (Shah, 2020, p. 23). Asset-based community development arose as a way to rebuild communities by shifting the focus from a deficit-view of low-income communities in community development programs to a strengths-based view (Kretzmann & McKnight, 1993). One of the dangers of a deficit-based view is that it positions community members as "fundamentally deficient victims incapable of taking charge of their lives and of their community's future" (Kretzmann & McKnight, 1993, p. 4). Community writing scholars have illustrated how a deficit-view can lead to communities being detrimentally perceived in terms of their struggles (Boyle-Baise & Efiom, 1999; Mitchell et al., 2012). As Cruz and Giles (2000) explained, taking a strengths-based view rather than a deficit-view is more beneficial: "Instead of asking what does a community need and focusing on its deficiencies, this approach asks what a community has that can be further developed and utilized by the community" (p. 31). Rather than focusing on the negative elements in communities, such as crime, violence, welfare dependency, and drugs, asset-based community development emphasizes recognizing the positive capacities of communities, such as creativity, local wisdom, and survival-motivated tactics.

Although well-intentioned, framing partnerships in a way that emphasizes responding to a problem or issue in the community can be stigmatizing and can cause harm or can even unwittingly promote a savior mentality. Community writing scholars Shane Bernardo and Terese G. Monberg (2019) noted that "savior narratives and community deficit narratives have been critiqued but are also ongoing, and what is often missing is a larger story of how these disparities came to be and continue" (p. 87). An asset-based approach is also a tool to mindfully challenge and confront our own scholarly bias as academics. We are traditionally trained to see disciplinary problems and to frame research as a response to a problem (whether that be something concrete, such as a pressing social problem like incarceration, or something abstract, such as a problem of representation in the field). Rather than situating our projects and programs as revolving around community needs or problems (a deficit, problem-based point of view), we can emphasize the "importance of utilizing local assets as key resources in tackling inequalities" (Harrison et al., 2019, Background section, para. 3). We can work on building relationships of mutual respect that promote interdependence between university and community—where "people can count on their neighbors and neighborhood resources for support and strength" (Kretzmann & McKnight, 1993, p. 27). Kretzmann and McKnight advise that a focus on a community's assets and resources "offers the most promising route toward successful community development" (p. 27).

Guiding Principle 2: We Value the Co-Creation of Knowledge With Our Community Partners

Is the project reciprocal? Is the project designed to co-create knowledge? Does the project bring the university and community together to share authority for knowledge creation? The second guiding principle foregrounds the co-creation of knowledge. Community-engaged partnerships involve both the university and the community partner's participation in generating new knowledge. This could look quite different from a "service" or "outreach" approach, which may involve the "delivery" of expertise, training, or service that travels in one direction from the university to the community. Barbara A. Holland (2005) observed, "Too often, faculty assume that in a campus-community partnership, the faculty role is to teach, the students' role is to learn, and the community partner's role is to provide a laboratory or set of needs to address or to explore" (p. 11). A focus on co-creation ensures that community participants are positioned as "coproducers of knowledge and practice rather than objects of study" (Costanza-Chock, 2014, p. 207). Inherent in the engaged scholarship model is the pursuit of knowledge "through the combining of academic knowledge and community-based knowledge, eliminating a hierarchy of knowledge and a one-way flow of knowledge outward from the college or university" (Campus Compact, n.d.-b, Defining Engaged Scholarship section).

As scholars in community engagement critique, our research has often been shaped by colonial ideas of ownership, control, and the pursuit of status, focusing more on gains for the university than on gains for the community (Hartman 2015; Mathieu 2005; Patel 2015; Saltmarsh & Hartley 2012; Shah 2020). As Shah (2020) has noted, colonial patterns reinforce "paternalistic views of communities that legitimize university control of funds, agents, and decisions in collaborations," and she has warned that these "patterns stretch back to the early days of community engagement and the community writing fields, and they will continue in the future if they are not interrupted" (p. 173).

Part of the work to decolonize partnerships rests in the politics of knowledge construction. As we work as a field to deepen community engagement, we must examine how narrowly we may have come to determine and evaluate our ways of knowing—for example, favoring expert or specialist knowledge over community knowledge. Privileging university-based knowledge and undervaluing community-based knowledge has deep consequences. It invalidates "the knowledges of community members, and thus makes deep partnership and the practice of collaborative knowledge production difficult" (Shah, 2020, p. 5). Part of our work moving forward includes how to orient our partnerships so that both community-based knowledge and university-based knowledge are truly valued in a context of partnership and reciprocity.

Community writing scholars have long noted the importance of building reciprocal relations with community partners (d'Arlach et al., 2009; Flower 2008; Lohr & Lindenman, 2018; Sandy & Holland 2006). Through this scholarship, we can better understand what defines the movement today and how to support it in our work. Lina D. Dostilio and her colleagues (2012) conducted a useful concept review of reciprocity in community engagement literature in which they examined three orientations to reciprocity in the field of university-community partnerships. The first orientation looked at reciprocity through the lens of *exchange*—when both parties participate in the interchange of benefits, resources, or actions. The second orientation examined reciprocity through the lens of *influence*—when both parties in the collaboration are iteratively changed due to being influenced by the participants and their contributed ways of knowing and doing. The last orientation saw reciprocity through the lens of *generativity*—a function of the collaborative relationship in which participants (who have or develop identities as co-creators) become and/or produce something new together that would not otherwise exist. This orientation may involve transformation of "individual ways of knowing and being or of the systems of which the relationship is a part" (Dostilio et al., 2012, p. 20).

A generative view of reciprocity aligns with notions of "thick" reciprocity—reciprocity that "emphasizes shared voice and power and insists upon collaborative knowledge construction and joint ownership of work processes and products" (Jameson et al., 2011, p. 264). "Thinner" reciprocity is demonstrated by the transactional, exchange-oriented relationship and grows "thicker" the more both parties engage in the "collaborative generation of knowledge, shared power, and joint ownership of the full scope of work processes and outcomes" (Janke, 2018, p. 12). A thicker, richer reciprocal approach means that partners are working to "share and shape ideas together in a generative and collaborative spirit" (Janke, 2018, p. 13).

To construct genuinely collaborative partnerships, "we need to consider the relationship-building process, which involves multiple parties, all of whom need to contribute to the construction of the relationship for it to be reciprocal" (Powell & Takayoshi, 2003, p. 417). Reciprocal relationship building calls for "an open and conscious negotiation of the power structures reproduced during the give-and-take interactions of the people involved in both sides of the relationship" (Cushman, 1996, p.16). This orientation shifts the position of communities from knowledge consumers to capable knowledge producers and acknowledges the inherent expertise that lies within communities. A generative reciprocal relationship may mean that both parties are not only learning *with* but *from* one another in a non-hierarchical process. A reciprocal relationship may also mean that power and authority are shared "in all aspects of the relationship, from defining problems, choosing approaches, addressing issues, developing the final products, and participating in assessment" (Saltmarsh et al., 2009, p.10). In an equity-based collaboration, we position ourselves as "stewards not of specific pieces of knowledge but rather of the productive and generative spaces that allow for finding knowledge" (Patel, 2015, p.79). By designing spaces for the discovery and co-creation of knowledge, we build capacity within our communities and gain insights that can inform our discipline as we strive to do better. These conversations are signposts for consideratixon regarding the co-creation of knowledge within writing partnerships.

Guiding Principle 3: We Are Committed to a Process of Transformative Change

Are the community's gains put first? Does the research project apply new knowledge to address issues in the community? Is the research impact collaboratively evaluated? Is the impact transformative? The third guiding principle entails collaboratively assessing impact and social change at the level of the partnership. It focuses on shifting from a relationship based on transaction to one based on transformation. Designing spaces for mutual knowledge creation and mutual benefit requires intentional framing of the research. A community-based approach asks both parties to define the topic at hand and frame the inquiry regarding the issue. How we first frame the research question (or the design question) not only establishes a research project but also plays a crucial role in limiting what can and cannot happen within our partnerships (discussed in more detail in Chapter 2 and Chapter 4). Community-engaged scholarship involves an approach to research that "moves away from emphasizing products (e.g., publications) to emphasizing impact" (Fitzgerald et al., 2012, p. 7). That is not to say that products and publications are not necessary but rather that we should prioritize a commitment to community impact throughout the process. This prioritization has not always been the case, as research on the effects of engagement on community partners is conspicuously lacking (Blouin & Perry, 2009; Cooks & Scharrer, 2006; Sandy & Holland 2006; Shah 2020). If we are to remain accountable to our partners, we "have to adjust our lines of inquiry and our discourse to be sure we are engaging with communities with every effort to partner mutually with, and to the equal benefit of, our communities" (Bortolin, 2011, p. 56). The CCCC Statement on Community-Engaged Projects in Rhetoric and Composition now urges scholars to focus on communities by providing "evidence of discernible, specific contributions such projects make to the public good" (Conference on

College Composition and Communication, 2016). By putting the community's gains first (over the university's gains and commitments, such as in our publications, grants, and even student learning outcomes), we can frame our research as "a process which builds community," and our "research can be viewed as community-building" (Checkoway, 2015, p. 139). We can learn what is possible in this enterprise by asking more focused questions that help us achieve the goals of both university and community partners.

Framing our research from a community-based perspective means that we can also evaluate our research from a community-based perspective. We can remain accountable to our partners by asking, "Did we engage in a process that builds community? Evaluation of our work can be grounded in a framework of alignment that values the building of trusting, mutually enriching relations with community partners. When the project cycle is near completion, we can ask, "Has there been an increase in net community assets? " (Cruz & Giles, 2000, p. 31). These questions can be set into motion from the beginning of the partnership as we align our resources around our shared goals. Just as knowledge can be co-constructed in research partnerships, we can collaboratively evaluate their outcomes. When both parties prioritize a commitment to community impact, they can

> design and implement the actions to be taken on the basis of their shared understanding of the problem. Together, the parties can develop plans of action to improve the situation together, and they evaluate the adequacy of what was done. (Greenwood, 2008, p. 327).

Further research into methods for evaluation are warranted since "a major voice that's missing . . . is whether the community partners feel like they're getting benefit out of a mutually-beneficial partnership" (Yates & Accardi, 2019, p.41). Community engagement scholar Kathleen Bortolin (2011) asked practitioners "to undertake more research focused on community voice, community perspective, and community outcomes" (p. 56). In answering that call, scholars are exploring evaluative approaches that have roots in reciprocal principles. Community partner evaluations of the projects and other forms of feedback from "community members might be immediately useful for community engagement coordinators, instructors, and administrators looking to understand community impact and improve programs to deepen reciprocity" (Shumake & Shah, 2017, p. 14). To better measure partnership outcomes, Shah (2020) recommended a participatory evaluation process, a form of "program evaluation that involves stakeholders in analyzing the effectiveness and impact of an initiative" (p. 144). Shumake & Shah (2017) further suggested that "inviting community members to contribute to student grading might . . . have the potential to be both a valid form of assessment and a method for better incorporating . . . reciprocity (p. 14). Stephen Danley and Gayle Christiansen (2019) proposed implementing community boards "as an oversight mechanism grounded in community that can address the often conflicting multi-dimensional ethical responsibilities within such partnerships from a community perspective" (p.8). There is a growing focus on how reciprocal evaluation methods such as partner evaluations, community grading, and community boards, help ensure that the requirements and expectations of both parties are met. These methods may also help ensure that our work is more inclusive and just.

We know that projects in community writing entail an enduring commitment to working with and within local communities. It takes time to build reciprocal relationships and to understand the nature and the possibilities of such work. Writing with communities is a form of slow media. Slow-media is the antithesis to a fast-paced, design-sprint ethos. Sasha Costanza-Chock (2020) has argued that

> start-up ideology, such as "move fast, break things" and "fail hard, fail fast," can become a justification for working styles that replicate broader structural inequality, when privileged student designers get to have a learning experience that involves making mistakes in the real world at the expense of community partners. (Preface section)

Like the slow food movement, the slow media movement is about making conscious decisions to consume and produce sustainable work that will help us grow, both in our classrooms and in our communities. Circulating disciplinary views suggest that engaged research should ground long-term faculty commitments in communities to build these relationships (Cushman 1996; Powell & Takayoshi 2003; Prell 2003; Taggart 2007). Powell & Takayoshi suggested that "thinking about the ethics of our research relationships will expand the ways we can envision the shape these relationships might take" (p. 398). To build stronger relationships with communities, partnerships "need to be viewed less as discrete, short-term efforts that function alongside the core work of the academy and more as mechanisms for making engagement an essential vehicle to accomplish higher education's most important goals" (Fitzgerald et al., 2012, p. 23). To work toward our higher-order objectives requires that we shift our view from project deliverables at the end of the semester toward more sustainable and long-term commitments. This means that our community partnerships might not necessarily be conducted, completed, or evaluated in one semester—what many, including myself, have often accepted as the default setting for a course project. Christina L. Prell (2003) argued that "long-term commitments allow scholars to understand better the needs of community clients and come up with well-planned, sustainable solutions to those needs" (p. 194). This might entail setting the expectations up front that students contribute to a larger conversation with the community partner and that their work is not necessarily to complete a project deliverable in a given semester; rather, their work is part of a more considerable, ongoing investment.

By intentionally framing our research as a long-term process that builds community, we can begin to do just that—reimagine our programs, our partnerships, even our discipline. As community writing scholar Jeff Grabill (2010) acknowledged, it is possible to frame engaged scholarship in a way that can "drive change within a department, program, or college in terms of how that activity is understood and valued" (p.20). Through this work, we can learn to build not only mutually beneficial partnerships but also mutually transformative ones. Building transformative relationships "requires the fostering of substantive shifts in institutional culture and academic practices" (Yates & Accardi, 2019, p. 34). Deep and lasting change is not a single end point but rather emerges over time "from an accountable, accessible, and collaborative process" (Costanza-Chock, 2020, Preface section). For deep and transformative change to occur, we must examine power and privilege in an intentional and reciprocal process. Dostilio and co-authors (2012) claimed that "the potential of reciprocity within these new spaces is generativity-oriented in that it opens the possibility for new and different ways of being, processes, and outcomes to emerge" (p. 25). These principles provide a starting framework for our goals and aims as we work with communities.

Chapter 2. How Might We Join With Community Partners in a Process of Inquiry That Embodies the Values of Mutuality and Reciprocity?

This chapter focuses on methods of collaboration in community-engaged partnerships. The approach to collaboration with partners will determine how new knowledge is produced by whom, for whom, and by what means. If the goal is to engage in the "mutually beneficial exchange of knowledge and resources in a context of partnership and reciprocity" (Commission on Public Purpose in Higher Education, n.d., Defining Community Engagement section) we will need methods that best enable that outcome. The guiding principles from Chapter 1 represent some emerging thoughts within the field of community writing. These principles can provide a framework for our goals and aims as we work with communities.

How can we best join with community partners in a process of inquiry that embodies these values? While there are many methods for facilitating projects with communities, including community-engaged research, participatory action research (PAR), service design, design-based research (DBR), assets-based community development (ABCD), and community-based participatory research (CBPR), this chapter will focus primarily on four design research methods for working with community partners:

- design thinking,
- co-design,
- design justice, and my own contribution,
- equity-based approaches in community writing.

Each of these collaborative methods entails a design research process where "people seek to understand, interpret and ultimately address a challenge or opportunity in their present reality by conceptually developing and creating things (e.g., spaces, physical products, services, infrastructures, policies etc.) that could create a (better) future reality" (Zamenopoulos & Alexiou, 2018, p.11). After a discussion of design thinking, co-design, and design justice, this chapter describes an equity-based approach to creating generative spaces in which communities and universities can collaborate in a research process specifically suited for the field of writing studies.

Design Thinking

When using design thinking, we start from a place of inquiry, whether the project engages *directly* with community members or *indirectly* with communities by working with nonprofit staff. Design thinking can be a valuable method to facilitate aspects of community-engaged projects with community partners. According to social scientist Herbert Simon (1981), "Everyone designs who devises courses of action aimed at changing existing situations into preferred ones" (p. 54). Emerging in the 1970s-1980s to describe designers' ways of knowing (Cross, 1982; Lawson, 1980; McKim, 1972), design thinking is an approach to creative problem solving that uses the lens of inquiry. The process typically includes a cycle of empathizing, defining, ideating, prototyping, and testing (Brown, 2009). The specific methods employed, however, are not as important as the overall process, which is grounded in understanding what is meaningful to the audience, discovering the audience's articulated and unarticulated needs and desires, imagining the world from the audience's perspective, and connecting with the audience around what is meaningful and valuable to them (Brown, 2009; Cross, 2011; Lockwood, 2009).

With its rhetorical, audience-based approach and its claims to demystify the design process, it is easy to understand how practitioners have taken up design thinking in the field of writing studies. James P. Purdy (2014) acknowledged the ties between design thinking and the writing process in his article "What Can Design Thinking Offer Writing Studies?" in which he examined the level of "comfort that many members of the field feel using the language of design to explain the writing practices they study, teach, and enact" (p. 613). Composition scholar Richard Marback (2009), drawing on the work of Richard Buchanan, called for "a fuller turn to design in composition studies" and argued for design as a way into "wicked problems"—complex cultural or social planning problems in the real world that are not inherently solvable (p. 400). Design thinking not only helps students understand and practice the process of inquiry, it also helps "students learn to practice a focused, coherent approach to collaborative invention" (Wible, 2020, p. 413). Applying design thinking methods to real-world projects allows students "to think in terms of collaborative responses" (Purdy, 2014, p. 631). Additionally, design thinking in the writing classroom can "facilitate students' engagement with writing in ways that lead them to see its value for their future" (Leverenz, 2014, p. 10).

Another benefit to the writing studies audience of the design thinking process is how it invites students to view issues through multiple points of view. In Scott Wible's (2020) article "Using Design Thinking to Teach Creative Problem Solving in Writing Courses," he noted,

> Common proposal and feasibility report assignments too often allow students to describe problems from their own self-interested perspectives, encourage them to move too quickly to proposing solutions, or allow them simply to import solutions used elsewhere or develop new solutions from the comfort of the classroom. (p. 421)

Design thinking tools offer students ways to engage with "other stakeholders in order to discover new insights on problems and to develop creative solutions"

(Wible, 2020, p. 421). Importantly, for some students, a community partner project might be the first time they are asked to create something that takes another's point of view into account.

Design thinking offers a roadmap for applying design research methods to a community partner project. Design thinking courses, workshops, and certificates are currently provided across disciplines and fields—through IDEO, an international design and consulting firm; Berkeley's Advanced Media Institute; the University of Pennsylvania's nursing program; and MIT's Sloan School of Management, to name just a few. Not just for the elite institutions, design thinking is promoted in a wide range of settings, from start-up incubators, nonprofit boot camps, and continuing education classes at community colleges. The Hasso Plattner Institute of Design at Stanford University (also known as the d.school) shares a Creative Commons "crash course" by way of a three-hour video session. Design thinking is now packaged as a popular commodity with online enrollment and flexible payment options. From universities to industry to nonprofits, design thinking has broad appeal.

It has been noted, however, that part of the appeal of design thinking is in the way it packages a designer's sensibilities and tools "for a non-designer audience by codifying their processes into a prescriptive, step by step approach to creative problem solving, claiming that it can be applied by anyone to any problems" (Jen, 2017, para. 5). While design thinking has many benefits, feminist scholars urge us to consider if this system can be everything to all people—and more importantly, should it be? Feminist scholars warn that the current pervasiveness of design thinking across sectors can ultimately be a colonizing project to the extent that it can be ascribed to anything and everything. Sociologist Ruha Benjamin (2019) claimed that "whether or not design speak acts out to colonize human activity, it is enacting a monopoly over creative thought and praxis" (p. 179) and asked, "What is gained and by whom in the process of submerging so much heterogeneity under the rubric of design?" (p. 176). Feminist designers and scholars claim that "the assumptions and methods of designers do not receive nearly as much critical engagement as they should" (Benjamin, 2019, p. 174). Part of what is at stake here is the question: *Who* is prioritized in the design process? Benjamin (2019) argued that such a wide focus on design could diminish

> the insights and agency of those who are discounted because they are not designers, capitalizing on the demand for novelty across numerous fields of action and coaxing everyone who dons the cloak of design into being seen and heard through the dominant aesthetic of innovation. (p. 179)

Design scholar Lucy Kimbell (2011) also acknowledged that "accounts of design thinking continue to privilege the designer, however empathetic, as the main agent in design" (p. 300). For example, in community-engaged projects, communities are often invited "to give their perspective and to give their feedback, but are otherwise left out of the design process" (Miller, 2017, para. 6). Hosting a community feedback session with community partners is not enough. As Meg Miller (2017) noted, Antionette Carroll, founder of the Creative Reaction Lab, has explained, "You cannot say that you are effectively addressing these issues if you are not including the people affected by them into your efforts, and giving them access to power" (para. 7). If we are committed to co-creation and putting the community first in our writing projects, we need to do more than host a feedback session—we need to join together with communities in a way that works to build on their ideas and visions.

Another critique of design thinking is its emphasis on problem solving. As discussed in Chapter 1, an asset-based approach favors the framing of community projects in terms of strengths rather than in the language of problems and solutions. Employing solutionist language can do more harm than good. Scholar Lee Vinsel (2017) has argued that using design thinking in courses conveys an "elitist, Great White Hope vision of change that literally asks students to imagine themselves entering a situation to solve other people's problems" (para. 37). Solutionist language can also give students an "unrealistic idea of design and the work that goes into creating positive change" (Vinsel, 2017, para. 36). When working in communities, we confront inherently complex and "wicked" issues—the consequences of inequitable and unjust systems. In Miller's (2017) article "Want to Fight Inequality? Forget Design Thinking," she claimed, "These systems are so embedded into history and society they are invisible to many, meaning there's no one simple thing to solve for" (para. 12). As Miller (2017) noted of Carroll, the founder of Creative Reaction Lab, she "prefers to use the word 'approaches' rather than 'solutions' . . . because it shows this is not a finite type of solution—it's flexible, it's agile" (para. 12). Similarly, Horst W. J. Rittel and Melvin M. Webber (1973) acknowledged that wicked problems are not inherently solvable, rather, "at best they are only re-solved over and over again" (p. 160). We must be mindful with our words; communities are not problems to be overcome or solutions to be sought. We too might take up the language of asset-based creative approaches in working with communities toward equity and justice in all aspects of the partnership.

Overall, design thinking can offer us valuable tools in community-engaged projects. However, what would be lost if we relied on design thinking (a system championed widely by industry in the global North) as our sole method of engagement for working with communities? As educator Sherri Spelic (2018) noted of design thinking, it suits "a certain kind of neoliberal enthusiasm for entrepreneurship and start-up culture. I question how well it lends itself to addressing social dilemmas fueled by historic inequality and stratification" (para. 18). A challenge for those working from a design thinking perspective will be moving from a limited feedback model to a working model that more deeply values social justice, reciprocity, and the co-creation of knowledge.

Co-Design

This section moves beyond design thinking to examine co-design as a method for community-engaged partnerships. Co-design is about "people designing together" and has roots in 1970s Scandinavian participatory design techniques (Sanders, 2002, p. 9). Co-design is an umbrella term used for a variety of collaborative approaches—such as co-operative design, open design, and service design—all attempting to involve stakeholders and use participatory means deeply. A key tenet of co-design is the building and deepening of shared collaboration between communities attempting to resolve a particular design challenge in a particular context. Co-design is used in both academia and professional practice as a term to indicate the sharing of power and the prioritizing of the community in the design research process (McKercher, 2020). It occurs over time and "requires a different kind of relation between people which incorporates trust, open and active communication and multiple learning" (Burkett, 2012, p. 8).

Co-design works to shift the power relationship between designers and participants from hierarchical to collaborative. In projects employing co-design, both parties are viewed as co-creators. Community writing scholar Thomas Deans (2010), in *Writing and Community Engagement: A Critical Sourcebook*, distinguished between (a) programs that write *for* the community, (b) programs that write *about* the community, and (c) programs that write *with* the community. Participatory methods firmly fall into the latter category, writing *with*, although as Deans acknowledged, the definite boundaries are not quite as distinct as they seem on paper. A key tenet of co-design is the view that "collaboration is more than just tapping into the individual knowledge that internal and external stakeholders possess. It is about discovering their unique, and collective perspectives on the systems in which they live, which makes it vital to create together" (Stratos Innovation Group, 2016, para. 3). In the co-design process, "the knowledge that stakeholders bring, is both explicit and tacit" (Langley et al., 2018, "What is co-design?" section). It is critical that community partners see the design research process as equitable and are seen, heard, and treated as leaders and decision-makers throughout the process. Communities are positioned as experts of their own lived experience within the process, and their voices become central to the project. We can value community voices by supporting their perspectives and stories in order to combat biases and assumptions and to "focus on strengths and resources that acknowledge but don't focus solely on disadvantage" (McKercher, 2020, p. 171). In working toward reciprocal relationships, there are many ways to approach meaningful co-creation in research with our partners; we can gather the information together, co-create design questions, share insights, and co-evaluate outcomes, to name a few. Co-design is a flexible approach; we can ask our partners how *they* would like to share power and authority when we begin.

Despite our well-meaning intentions, the field of community writing acknowledges the work that is still left to be done: "Social, cultural, racial, economic, and educational inequalities make it difficult for instructors to bring the ideals of reciprocity into practice" (Shumake & Shah, 2017, p. 6). Saying that we value co-creation with communities does not lessen the "unequal power dynamics that commonly exist between students and community members, especially when students are from privileged or elite backgrounds" (Shumake & Shah, 2017, p. 6). Additionally, Kelly A. McKercher (2020) argued that in order "to continue shifting power it's critical that we evaluate the success of co-design processes and their outputs (e.g., a service or policy) against whether they create value, from the perspective of the people they're supposed to benefit" (p. 219). Co-design is the act of creating *with* "stakeholders . . . specifically within the design development process to ensure the results meet their needs and are usable" (Stratos Innovation Group, 2016, para. 6). A co-design process is determined successful if the products or services "create value for the people they are intended to benefit" (McKercher (2020) p. 18).

In a university context, regardless of the amount of scaffolding provided by the educator, co-designing with communities can be a daunting endeavor with multiple moving parts. Many co-designed projects are not usable by community partners despite our best efforts. To this point, Shah (2020) followed up on 43 student projects created by various professional writing classes for nonprofits and found that fewer than one third of them were usable by the organization without alterations, and according to her, the outcomes of the projects, such as "brochures, promotional videos, data reports, or website plans . . . were not readily usable" (p. 67). Moreover, in her interviews, she discovered that the nonprofits

> discussed an ideal student group that would have the confidence to propose fresh ideas rather than merely follow the directions of the nonprofit staffer, to interact as colleagues rather than students—demonstrating assertiveness but also responsiveness—and to communicate about problems as they arose. They wanted students to participate in many ways as professional consultants, rather than as pupils. In sum, they wanted students to play an active role in the knowledge network. (Shah, 2020, p. 84)

Ultimately, the decision to implement the project as submitted by the students lies with the community partner. If there is still time in the semester, perhaps there is a chance to synthesize more feedback for revision. If the semester is over, there may be a chance to develop the project (and the community partner relationship) with another group of students in a different semester. One of the many challenges is "learning how to successfully navigate the 'messiness' of an inclusive design process that takes everyone's lived experience seriously" (Costanza-Chock, Preface section). When our research is grounded in co-creation methods, we can make more significant strides toward designing *with* our partners, not just *for* our partners—and having those designs actually be useful to the community. In this way, co-design is more than a research process—it is a movement toward more just and equitable partnerships.

Design Justice

If we want to change inequitable and unjust systems, first we need to do the work to understand them. It is not enough to join with community partners in a process of inquiry that embodies the values of mutuality and reciprocity—unless we are also examining the reasons why "not everyone starts with the same resources or experiences the same barriers to success" (Mission Investors Exchange, 2019, para. 10). In our work with communities, we must seek to understand the following: "Why are these communities in need? Why are these communities similar in demographics regardless of where they are located across the country? Why have the needs been consistent for several decades?" (Campus Compact, n.d.-a, para. 1). Centering equity in our work with communities means that we learn from those with experience in historically underinvested neighborhoods. The National Equity Project (n.d.) has argued that

> our public systems (education, healthcare, criminal justice, housing, etc.) were not created to produce equal outcomes or experiences for everyone. These structures—past and present— maintain inequity by design. These inequitable systems were not created by accident and they will not be undone by chance. New, liberating systems must be designed with conscious intention and a shared vision for a desired future state. (We Believe section)

When we center equity and justice in our projects, we begin to do the work of understanding why our current systems perpetuate inequity by design. Unless we are doing this work, our efforts toward mutuality and reciprocity are little more than lip service since "one cannot reciprocally value what one does not understand" (Davis et al., 2017, p. 49). Centering equity and justice in our work with community partners offers a way to diversify our theory building—"a vital project for the field of community writing" that seeks to "highlight inequalities between university and community" (Shah, 2020, p. 10). Charting a new path toward justice means creating spaces where "power, privilege, and oppression are actively and intentionally considered" (Dostilio et al., 2012, p. 25). The power dynamics that uphold oppression are embedded, in fact *designed* into, the very systems we want to change. Part of our work will necessarily be about how "systems of oppression, inequality, inequity are by design; therefore, they can and *must* be redesigned" (Creative Reaction Lab, 2019, para. 3).

In their recent book *Design Justice: Community-Led Practices to Build the Worlds We Need*, Costanza-Chock (2020) described the design justice movement as "a growing community of practice that aims to ensure a more equitable distribution of design's benefits and burdens; meaningful participation in design decisions; and recognition of community-based, Indigenous, and diasporic design traditions, knowledge, and practices" (Introduction section). Design justice works to employ collaborative practices to prioritize people who have been historically underinvested by design. It is a community-focused approach that intentionally asks "how design reproduces and/or challenges the matrix of domination (white supremacy, heteropatriarchy, capitalism, ableism, settler colonialism, and other forms of structural inequality)" (Costanza-Chock, 2020, Introduction section). According to design justice practitioners, "We have an ethical imperative to systemically advance the participation of marginalized communities in all stages of the technology design process; through this process, resources and power can be more equitably distributed" (Costanza-Chock, 2018, p.6).

Critical discussions centering on design justice originated at a session titled "Generating Shared Principles for Design Justice" at the 2015 Allied Media Conference in Detroit, facilitated by designers Una Lee and Wesley Taylor, in which

> the hope was to start shaping a shared definition of "design justice"—as distinguished from "design for social impact" or "design for good," which are well intentioned but because they are not driven by principles of justice can be harmful, exclusionary, and can perpetuate the systems and structures that give rise to the need for design interventions in the first place. How could we redesign design so that those who are normally marginalized by it, those who are characterized as passive beneficiaries of design thinking, become co-creators of solutions, of futures?" (Design Justice Network, 2016, para. 2)

The Design Justice Network officially began the following year at the 2016 Allied Media Conference through a network gathering organized by Lee, Taylor, Victoria Barnett, Carlos Garcia, and Nontsikelelo Mutiti. Network gatherings at the Allied Media Conference have established opportunities for "a . . . way to connect with other people who share your values around a shared purpose or cause" (Allied Media Conference, n.d., FAQ 4). Today, the Design Justice Network includes over 2,000 "designers, developers, technologists, scholars, educators, community organizers, and many others who are working to examine and transform design values, practices, narratives, sites, and pedagogies so that they don't continue to reinforce interlocking systems of structural inequality" (Costanza-Chock, 2020, Preface) The members of the Design Justice Network produce zines, organize local nodes, host programs, trainings, reading groups, and working groups, and continue to coordinate an ongoing track at the annual Allied Media Conference. Their goal is to actively dismantle, rather than unintentionally reinforce, what Patricia Hill Collins (1990) termed "the matrix of domination" (p. 556). As Costanza-Chock (2020) explained,

> For many people from marginalized groups, the ways that the matrix of domination is both reproduced by and produces designed objects and systems at every level— from city planning and the built environment to everyday consumer technologies

to the affordances of popular social media platforms—generates
a constant feeling of alterity (feeling of being othered). (Design
Values section)

The goals of the design justice movement are to grow a community of practice that works, not to limit or exclude design choices but rather to offer a robust framework that can be used "as a prism through which we generate a far wider rainbow of possible choices, each better tailored to reflect the needs of a specific group of people" (Costanza-Chock, 2020, Directions for Future Work section).

Achieving reciprocity in community partnerships "requires that all involved maintain their integrity to their own perspective, and bring their unique perspective to the project, sharing openly so that all may benefit from others' knowledge; the process is one in which diversity is truly a strength" (Davis et al., 2017, p. 49). By centering equity and justice in our work, we are better prepared to value multiple ways of knowing and being. Pursuing research together in reciprocal partnership means "providing a way for people to share their knowledge from the margins" (Shah, 2020, p. 26). Our community partners hold unique insight (not in spite of, but) because of their positionality. Valuing experiential knowledge, lived experience, and counter-storytelling (narratives that counter dominant assumptions) are some ways to prioritize underinvested voices in community-university partnerships. There is a growing community of practitioners—people, agencies, universities, and organizations—who work daily to leverage the power of design for equity. The design justice movement is just one of many spaces that reflect the values of anti-racism, anti-oppression, and justice. These include the following organizations:

- And Also Too's mission is to "facilitate the co-creation of art, design, media, and technology to support movements for justice and liberation" (para. 1).
- Boston University Center for Antiracist Research's mission "is to convene researchers and practitioners from various disciplines to figure out novel and practical ways to understand, explain, and solve seemingly intractable problems of racial inequity and injustice" (Boston University Center for Antiracist Research, n.d., para. 1).
- Creative Reaction Lab's mission is "to educate, train, and challenge Black and Latinx youth to become leaders in designing healthy and racially equitable communities" (n.d., para. 1).
- Highlander Research and Education Center's mission is to catalyze "grassroots organizing and movement building in Appalachia and the South" (n.d., para 1).
- Hyphen-Labs is an international team of women of color "driven to create engaging ways to explore planetary-centered design. In the process they challenge conventions and stimulate conversations, placing collective needs and experiences at the center of evolving narratives" (n.d., para. 1).

- Ida B. Wells JUST Data Lab's mission is to join Princeton University "students, educators, activists, and artists. . . . to rethink and retool data for justice" (The Center for Digital Humanities at Princeton, n.d., para. 1).
- Research Action Design's mission is to "co-design tools, develop technology, and conduct essential research grounded in the needs and leadership of communities" (n.d., para. 2).

Equity-Based Approaches in Community Writing

While the previous three approaches to design research have their respective merits, none were explicitly created for writing partnerships. Additionally, approaching writing collaborations using only one of these methods may permit critical gaps that unintentionally threaten to undermine the work being attempted. For example, design thinking without the balance of a social justice framework could potentially perpetuate oppressive systems. Thus, here I introduce what I call equity-based approaches in community writing that synthesize assets from the previous methods discussed into a single, practical approach tailored for use in community writing.

Design research methods often employ an iterative feedback process, or what action research perennially (at least for the last 75 years) depicts as "spiral steps that form 'a circle of planning, action and fact finding about the result of the action" (Lewin, 1946, p. 52). Typically, the "circle of planning" is represented as a cyclical or hexagonal model with arrows indicating the action steps—a tidy package codified by a step-by-step procedure for the research. Although these visual models are ubiquitous and easy to understand, they are not always realistic, nor do they always represent what the collaborative process actually looks like. We know community writing can be messy, complex, "wicked" work that does not always adhere to a tidy step-by-step process. As Maggie Gram (2019) wrote, "to address a wicked problem is to look for its roots—and there's no hexagon map for getting there" (para. 64). My approach to community writing looks more like Figure 2.1.

The process represented in Figure 2.1 is a flexible and accommodating approach to writing and designing with community partners. In astronomy, the pole star positioned at the top of the illustration serves as a guide much like a compass would. In the northern hemisphere, the pole star never rises or sets and is visible any time of year. In this illustration, the pole star represents aspiring concepts such as social justice, reciprocity, and transformative change. These are the higher-order goals of our community-university partnerships. This pole star guides our work with communities and informs our on-the-ground tactics and decisions as we chart our path. Even if we are not always perfect at living up to all of them all of the time, we are actively engaging with these goals, and they can guide our work.

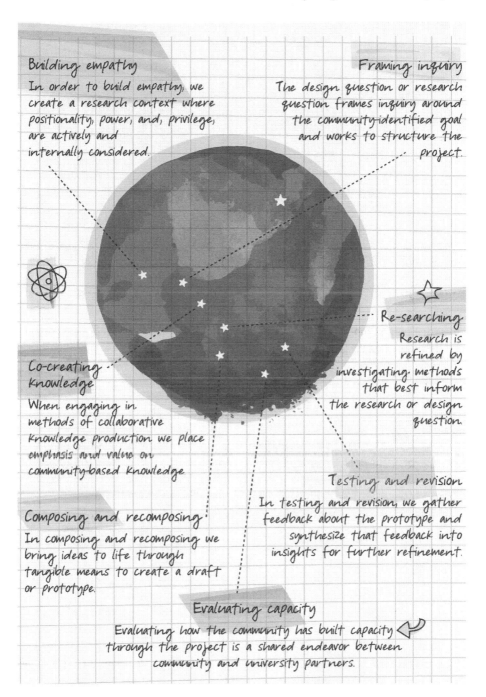

Building empathy
In order to build empathy, we create a research context where positionality, power, and, privilege, are actively and internally considered.

Framing inquiry
The design question or research question frames inquiry around the community-identified goal and works to structure the project.

Co-creating knowledge
When engaging in methods of collaborative knowledge production we place emphasis and value on community-based knowledge.

Re-searching
Research is refined by investigating methods that best inform the research or design question.

Composing and recomposing
In composing and recomposing we bring ideas to life through tangible means to create a draft or prototype.

Testing and revision
In testing and revision, we gather feedback about the prototype and synthesize that feedback into insights for further refinement.

Evaluating capacity
Evaluating how the community has built capacity through the project is a shared endeavor between community and university partners.

Figure 2.1. Equity-based approaches in community writing

Buddhist teacher Thich Nhat Hanh (2008) has used a similar analogy when discussing mindfulness practices. His teaching has included the idea that the goal of mindfulness practice is "not to be perfect but simply to be mindful of ourselves, even when we make mistakes," and he continued,

> If you are lost in a forest at night, you can follow the North Star
> to find your way out. You follow the North Star, but your goal
> is to get back home; it's not to arrive at the North Star. (Hanh,
> 2008, p. 62)

Similarly, the goal here is "not to arrive at the North Star"—it is "to get back home"— to do better work with our partners to build more just and transformative worlds.

In Figure 2.1, below the pole star there are seven stars that depict the asterism known throughout the world by various names, including the Big Dipper, bear, plough, rudder, and sages. Metaphorically, these stars can be viewed not as linear steps in a process but as approaches or possibilities for engagement that center equity when collaborating with communities. These approaches are discussed in more detail below and are put into practice in a case study in the next chapter.

Building Empathy

To build empathy, we create a research context where positionality, power, and privilege are actively considered. Empathy is an essential part of the research process, as it "is the active attempt to understand another person's perspective by imagining how you would feel, think, or act if put in their situation" (Creative Reaction Lab, 2018, p. 19). In building empathy, we can examine how our own identities, values, biases, assumptions, and relationships to power and privilege impact how we engage with ourselves, each other, and the communities with whom we work. Charting a path toward justice means creating a research context where positionality, power, and privilege are actively and internally considered. The University of Pennsylvania's Weingarten Learning Resources Center provides materials for students and faculty on positionality in the context of research ethics. In one blog post, the Weingarten Learning Resources Center (2017) noted that "power dynamics flow through every vein of the research process" and stated that "it is our ethical duty to intentionally and mindfully attend to our role(s) in the contextual power interplay of the research process" (para. 1). We must be intentional about creating spaces to critically reflect with students on how our positionalities both cohere and diverge from our research inquiries. Part of this work entails examining our positionality and asking, "How does my positionality recognize, honor, and or problematize notions of difference (politics, economics, class, race, ethnicity, citizenship, legality, age, ability, education, sexuality, gender, or religion) as a conceptual praxis of analysis for my research context?" (Weingarten Learning Resources Center, 2017, Bullet point 5). In the process of building empathy, we examine how our own identities, values, biases, assumptions, and relationships to power and privilege impact how we engage with ourselves, each other, and the communities with whom we work.

Empathy alone, however, is not enough to shift power or to change systems. Technologist Tatiana Mac (2020) has emphasized the need for trust and compassion to access empathy, arguing,

> Instead of trying to feel something we can't truly know to validate it, we should *trust* others' experiences. We can offer *compassion*, which doesn't require our own understanding in order to validate it as being real and worthy of attention. (paras. 8–9)

Additionally, the Creative Reaction Lab (2018) has argued for the need to build humility in order to access empathy, noting that an equity-centered approach "requires the humility to acknowledge where our assumptions and biases lie and the empathy to observe and listen with suspended judgment" (p. 19). Being vulnerable, experiencing discomfort, admitting mistakes, acknowledging that you don't know, learning together, sharing power—these are some ways to create a culture of co-creation and collective learning. More opportunities for building empathy in the classroom are offered in Appendix A: Positionality Activity.

Framing Inquiry

The design question, or research question, frames inquiry around the community-identified goal and works to structure the project. Our partnerships are based on a community-driven desire to build capacity or create change. We can continually inquire about the community partner's goals and work to collaborate with our partner as an ally. The design question frames inquiry around the community-identified goal and works to structure the project. A design question is a clear statement about a phenomenon of interest, a condition to be improved upon, an issue to be explored, or a question that exists in theory or practice for the partner's organization. An essential key to successful partnerships is sharing a vision to which we are all mutually committed. The purpose and vision of the project is established when we intentionally frame inquiry with our partners. Research questions and design questions are examined in more detail in the next two chapters.

Co-Creating Knowledge

When engaging in methods of collaborative knowledge production, we place emphasis and value on community-based knowledge. The National Equity Project (n.d.) has contended, "Co-creation acknowledges that we build *with* and not *for* others—we invite, engage and design solutions and co-produce knowledge in partnership" (We Believe section). When engaging in collaborative knowledge production methods, we emphasize and value community-based knowledge—that is, knowledge, stories, and expertise arising from the community. This entails actively decolonizing spaces for our work with communities in a way "that re-envisions and develops knowledges and knowledge systems (epistemologies) that have been silenced and colonized" (Zavala, 2016, The Decolonial Project section). Epistemological diversity can guide our work with communities. Not only do we value the embodied, tacit knowledge within the community, we can stand along-side our partners in their goals to envision "new ways of seeing and being in the world" (Zavala, 2016, The Decolonial Project section). As our projects privilege diverse ways of knowing, it is necessary to often connect with the community partner for consistent input, feedback, and insights. It is imperative that "com-munity members are seen and treated as leaders and decision-makers throughout the process" (Creative Reaction Lab, 2018, p. 33). In co-creation, we make greater strides toward designing *with* our partners, not *for* our partners—and having the projects we create ultimately be useful to the community.

Re-searching

Research· is refined by investigating methods that best inform the research or design question. A well-defined research or design question posed in the fram-ing inquiry phase will point to systematic investigation aimed at contributing to knowledge gained through careful consideration, observation, and study of our phenomenon of interest. Investigation will help to identify patterns and trends as well as to illuminate gaps or unknowns. There is an iterative nature to research—we often look for our phenomenon of interest and then must look again. Eventu-ally, the research is refined by "progressively developing more specific knowledge about a particular situation, and more specific descriptions of the plausible solu-tions that would create a future envisaged reality" (Sanders, 2002, p. 11). Research methods might also include ideation techniques, such as public brainstorming sessions and round robins, or more traditional scholarly and academic meth-ods, such as annotated bibliographies, surveys, interviews, and data collection. Research-based media activities are examined further in Chapter 4.

Composing and Recomposing

In composing and recomposing, we bring ideas to life through tangible means by creating a draft or prototype. Prior to this, we built momentum and a clear path forward once we began conducting research, and a leading idea emerged from the research phase. The composing phase is the process of making or bringing this leading idea to life—whether we are writing a first draft of a report or build-ing a prototype or model (such as constructing a visual wireframe for a website, a mockup for a social media campaign, a sketch for a logo, or a storyboard for a video). Eventually, this tangible act of composing will result in a prototype or a draft of a deliverable—or it will bring us back to the drawing board to conduct more research and begin the process of recomposing (composing again or differently). Costanza-Chock (2020) has noted that "narrowing down from big concepts to working prototypes within the available time can be very difficult. Part of the educator's role is to guide teams through this process with clear expectations and firm deadlines" (Design Pedagogies section).

Testing and Revision

We gather feedback about the prototype or draft in testing and revision, and we synthesize that feedback into insights for further refinement. With our prototype in hand, we can connect with our partners to determine the viability of our ideas and how to build on existing resources. Discussions, demonstrations, evaluation metrics, surveys, screenings, conversations, usability tests, conference rooms, virtual meetings, and coffee hours all are opportunities for feedback. As Costanza-Chock has reflected,

> Getting a prototype in front of real-world users early on in the design process is fundamental to making design more accessible. This is crucial because it helps to validate assumptions, reveal faulty thinking, and allow the team to iterate on the selected concept. (Design Pedagogies section)

Here we learn if the prototype-in-progress meets our partner's vision, and we can synthesize feedback from our partner into insights for further drafting and revision. Testing and revising is an interwoven process that happens throughout the project lifecycle. Sometimes revision means re-seeing the project from a new perspective and then rebuilding accordingly.

Evaluating Capacity

Evaluating how the community has built capacity through the project is a shared endeavor between community and university partners. In our work with community partners, we must prioritize the community throughout the process, including sharing and assessing insights after the project cycle is finished. When the project phase is complete, we can ask, "Did we engage in a process that builds community?" (Checkoway, 2015, p. 139). Ideally, the community partner would be involved in this evaluation. We can ask:

- Did the community partners improve capacity by adopting new habits, strategies, or skills for advancing change?
- Did we build a trusting, mutually enriching relationship together as co-creators?
- How can we best elicit community voices and perspectives in the project evaluation?

- How can we better work toward a collaborative evaluation process together?

Costanza-Chock (2020) proposed a three-part evaluation process to use when working with communities: "Who participated in the design process? Who benefited from the design? And who was harmed by the design?" (Directions for Future Work section). When someone says or does something to cause harm to someone, to marginalize someone, to make an assumption, to not listen well, to insist on doing something "our" way, to believe that we are "right," to issue a misinformed comment or judgment, to reject information that contradicts our beliefs, to uphold the status quo—these are just a few of the ways that we may do harm.

The Equity Design Collaborative (n.d.) defines design as "the intention (and unintentional impact) behind an outcome" (Design section). Thus, we should be held responsible for both the intentional and unintentional impacts of our design projects. Engaging in an opportunity for continuous improvement, for humility, for recognizing where we may cause harm creates an opportunity for us to consider the potential unintentional impacts of design. A project evaluation can help us attend to the unintentional impacts of the design process. Recognizing where in the course of a partnership we might have caused harm allows for accountability—and creates the possibility for transformation to occur.

When a community partner is harmed, trust declines. McKercher (2020) contended that "courageous conversations are vital" (p. 112). Can we be better prepared to hold deeper (and more courageous) conversations with our partners? Over time, as our community-university relationships develop, deeper and more honest discussions can take place. adrienne maree brown (2017) argued for adopting emergent strategy—that is, a strategy through which we can "intentionally change in ways that grow our capacity to embody the just and liberated worlds we long for" (p. 3). brown (2017) recommended that we "move at the speed of trust. Focus on critical connections more than critical mass—build the resilience by building the relationships" (p. 42). BlackSpace (n.d.), in The BlackSpace Manifesto, advised that partners "grow trust and move together with fluidity at whatever speed is necessary" (para. 5). Building trust is slow and transformational work, and we must be prepared to accept a lack of immediate gratification.

This flexible approach for conducting design research with communities can point us toward more just and equitable partnerships. Intentionally centering equity and justice when co-creating with communities requires us to redesign both mindsets and infrastructures to share power and decision-making with our partners.

Chapter 3. How Might We in the Writing Classroom Engage in Community-Building Approaches That Pursue Social Justice via Emerging Media?

The promise of social justice in the community writing classroom is the opportunity to work alongside partners whose intent is to create more equitable, socially just worlds. That said, social justice is a potential, a possibility—not something inherently found in all community-engaged writing projects. Drawing from the scholarship of Frey & Bohnet (1996), Jones et al. (2016) claimed that social justice research in a technical communication context can "amplify the agency of oppressed people—those who are materially, socially, politically, and/or economically under-resourced (p. 2). According to Kari M. Grain and Darren E. Lund (2016), the social justice turn in the writing classroom is accompanied by "a pedagogy that encounters injustice and divisiveness as it occurs in local and global communities" (p. 46). In "The Technical Communicator as Advocate: Integrating a Social Justice Approach in Technical Communication," Jones argued, "A social justice perspective must not be purely descriptive but actively integrated into the research and pedagogy of our field in a way that promotes social change on a broader level" (Jones, 2016, p. 349). Community-engaged projects have the potential to "integrate social justice into research and pedagogy within the field" and entail "critical reflection and action that promotes agency for the marginalized and disempowered" (Jones, 206, p. 342). Both critical reflection and action are necessary components of a socially just pedagogy in the writing classroom. Although the case for the social justice turn has been made in the literature, "few resources exist to help teachers explicitly address diversity and social justice in the technical communication classroom" (Jones et al., 2016, p. 242). Jones and co-authors (2016) warned that

> without targeted teaching resources, educators will continue to struggle—or worse, fail altogether—to equip the next generation of technical communication scholars and practitioners for the complex work of recognizing, acting within, and shaping issues of social justice and diversity. (p. 242)

Providing an opportunity to critically examine how race, class, and gender shape identity is a necessary starting place in the community-engaged writing classroom, as both students and teachers will undoubtedly confront socialized and entrenched notions of power and privilege within the context of this work. Examining our positionality is a part of building empathy in the research process and includes looking at how we are positioned (by ourselves, by others, by particular discourse communities) in relation to multiple, relational social processes of difference (gender, class, race, ethnicity, age, education, ability, religion, nationality, sexuality). Doing this work means taking a critical look at how we are each differently positioned in hierarchies of power and privilege. Collins (1990) argued that "people experience and resist oppression on three levels: the level of personal biography; the group or community level of the cultural context created by race, class, and gender; and the systemic level of social institutions" (p. 223). Additionally, Collins (1990) acknowledged that "each individual derives varying amounts of penalty and privilege from the multiple systems of oppression which frame everyone's lives" (p. 229).

Alongside critical reflection, active participation in a partnership is the second piece of a social justice pedagogy in a writing studies context. As Jones (2016) noted, "Community-based research allows teachers to pair with specific communities and work collaboratively to address or solve a problem that directly impacts the community" (p. 355). In community writing partnerships, we join forces with grassroots, community-based organizations and nonprofits fighting for justice. Empathy and humility serve us well as we strive to "(a) redress colonial influences on perceptions of people, literacy, language, culture, and community and the relationship therein and (b) support the coexistence of cultures, languages, literacies, memories, histories, places, and space—and encourage respectful and reciprocal dialogue between and across them" (Jones, 2016, p. 350).

One of the challenges of community-university partnerships is redressing the university's historic devaluation of nonwestern forms of knowledge and value systems. Anthropologist Arturo Escobar (2018) questioned whether universities are too ensconced in colonial systems to truly value community-based knowledge, and he acknowledged that formal educational systems, such as universities, have historically devalued multiple forms of local knowledge and meaning-making. He asked, "Can the university really move beyond its inexorable ties to the cultures of expertise?" (Escobar, 2018, p. 233). While arguing for a decolonized approach to design, Escobar (2018) questioned whether those in the university can truly design and learn "within grassroots cultures" (p. 223). There is often a stark difference between what universities practice and what they preach. According to a Leading and Learning Initiative report written by Erica Kohl-Arenas and coauthors (2020), "Institutions often claim to value community-engaged, collaborative, diverse, social change, and equity-based work in their missions yet internally organize around the norms and structures that reward individualism, competition, prestige, assimilation, and the status quo" (p. 3). If our goals are to engage in co-creation (see the Co-creating Knowledge section in this chapter) in a research process that values multiple ways of knowing and being, then we must actively work to locate, integrate, and value those ways of knowing and being in our community-engaged partnerships.

In that light, the social justice turn must be accompanied by the decolonial turn in writing studies. Decolonial scholars work to "build a foundation, a history of local knowledges and meaning-making practices" while highlighting "the colonialist legacies that inform the management and control of knowledges and subjectivities in literacy, composition, and rhetoric curricula" (García & Baca, 2019, p. 3). Decolonial scholars focus on collaborative and place-based practices that honor plurality as it shifts power and perspectives away from an established colonial center. To do this work, we need better tools to use—better ways to understand and perform the co-construction of knowledge between community and university. As Walter D. Mignolo (2007) argued, "If knowledge is colonized, one of the tasks ahead is to decolonize knowledge" (p. 451). We must interrogate our acceptance of our widely held colonial modes of thinking as the default modes. This might entail finding new possibilities in our partnerships that do not continue to serve and reproduce further oppression. Along these lines, Angela M. Haas (2012) argued that "for decolonial ideologies to emerge, new rhetorics must be spoken, written, or otherwise delivered into existence (p. 287). Decolonial work seeks "to change the terms as well as the contents of knowledge production" (García & Baca, 2019, p. 15). Mignolo (2007) claimed that delinking "leads to decolonial epistemic shift and brings to the foreground other epistemologies, other principles of knowledge and understanding, and consequently, other economy, other politics, other ethics" (p. 453). As Romeo García and Damián Baca (2019) argued, "The dangerous and radical possibility of the decolonial turn is the fact of its foundation's being based on the stories, epistemologies, thoughts and feelings of the anthropoi" (p. 15)—that, is of local communities operating within local meaning-making frameworks.

Practicing decolonial methods alongside our students and community partners, we can continue to change the terms on which we do the work. As García and Baca (2019) argued, the decolonization of knowledge production and meaning-making also needs to be accompanied by the "prospective task of contributing to build a work in which many worlds could exist" (p. 23). This entails a commitment to "honor and uplift traditional, indigenous, and local knowledge and practices" (Costanza-Chock, 2020, Introduction section). When we understand our partner's stories of hope, survival, and resistance as a foundation for our partnerships in communities, we might begin to do the work of dismantling oppression while at the same time working toward more just and equitable futures in what García and Baca (2019) termed a "spirit of pluralversality, which imagines humanity in difference" (p. 23).

Projects with Emerging Media

When combined with a community-engaged, socially just pedagogy, the study of emerging media can connect writing students with a network of publics and counterpublics, including activist groups and grassroots organizations—some of which may reside right in our own neighborhoods. Mathieu (2005) acknowledged that "by exploring and taking part in the public works of activists and writers in the streets, teachers and students of composition have much to learn and contribute to public discourse" (p. 28). The study of media in a community-writing context connects students with audiences and issues well beyond the classroom walls. In this book, the term "media" encompasses digital media, new media, multimedia, emerging media, and transmedia. Henry Jenkins has written prolifically about media education in the 21st-century and about fostering media literacies that focus on collaboration, networking, community, public voice, active participation, and democratic dialogue. These skills build on the foundations of traditional literacy that have traditionally been part of a literacy curriculum, such as research skills, technical skills, and critical analysis skills. In one publication, Jenkins and his co-authors (2016) observed that "we have seen an expansion of the communicative and organizational resources available to everyday people (and grassroots organizations) as we become more and more accustomed to using networked communications toward our collective interests" (p. 3).

A commitment to community building and civic action offers faculty and students opportunities to address immediate real-world issues right in our neighborhoods. When we view our work as a form of community-building, students and faculty can partner with communities to create new knowledge about communication practices and promote that knowledge transfer to school, workplace, and community contexts. The power of emerging media can be harnessed to suit the specific visions of communities, and we can use it as we work with our partners toward the social change that so many of us desire. This is a cultural shift, as well as a technological one. This is not just about the technology; it is about understanding the culture that emerging communication technologies enable—a culture of change-making.

Opportunities abound to work collaboratively with partners to understand how community writing teachers can employ emerging media to engage powerfully with communities, allies, stakeholders, and policymakers. We can accomplish this work in a range of academic courses, such as ones called

- community literacy
- decolonial studies
- design justice
- digital composition
- digital humanities
- digital publishing
- feminist media
- grant writing
- literacy activism
- multimedia writing

- nonprofit communication
- organizational writing
- professional writing
- public composition
- public rhetorics
- social media
- technical writing
- visual rhetorics
- web design
- writing in the public interest
- writing with communities
- writing studies

Although worthwhile, it is not necessary to have an entire course devoted to such work. A single hands-on project within a course can put theory into practice with a community partner. For example, in a technical writing course, a class project could create a social media campaign or a website for a nonprofit organization. Engaging in a media project with a community partner is a way to help organizations grow, making them even more effective at creating change in our communities. Community writing projects are a "power-up" for local organizations. Just as the Super Mushrooms in the Super Mario Bros. video game give players heightened powers, each community writing project amplifies an organization's goals and objectives by adding benefits and building capacities that were not there before. This process provides our community partners with the tools and strategies they are looking for to create a more effective, lasting change. Discussed next are three approaches to working with community partners on course projects that pursue social justice via emerging media.

Production-Oriented

When community partners build capacity with emerging media platforms and literacies, they can make a significant impact with modest resources—becoming more effective in their work and their reach as they challenge injustices and systemic inequalities. A production-oriented project is sometimes the most direct and immediate way to work with partners to create change. Some production-oriented media projects include

- producing materials for advocacy campaigns,
- developing and designing websites,
- creating graphics and logos,
- engaging in photography and visual storytelling,
- analyzing and visualizing data,

- writing and editing blog posts and newsletters,
- creating content and working with editorial calendars,
- filming and editing promotional videos,
- scripting and filming educational videos, or
- crafting event promotion materials.

Training-Oriented

A community writing project may involve hands-on media-based training at the partner's request —whether that be training in learning a new platform or training to better engage local audiences and discourse communities on platforms already in use. Students learning about emerging media can lead training sessions. They can also follow up with partners to reinforce the training since "those who make a practice of regularly producing and circulating their own media improve their skills and abilities over time" (Costanza-Chock, 2014, p. 198). Not only do media-based training-oriented projects offer community partners new technical and rhetorical skills, but also they provide new literacies that strengthen "awareness of ourselves as actors who have the ability to shape and transform the world, as well as of the structural (systemic) forces that stand in our way" (Costanza-Chock, 2014, p. 207). Some examples that could build capacity for communities might include

- providing a hands-on tutorial for a media platform such as WordPress or Squarespace,
- hosting a digital storytelling workshop where both community and university participate in the co-creation of knowledge, or
- demonstrating how to record interviews or podcasts.

Research-Oriented

Nonprofit and community-based organizations rely on strategic communication to create social change. When conducting media research with partners, student consultants consider practices in the field and conduct research to develop tailored recommendations and tactics to drive online engagement. While working through research-oriented projects, students learn useful platform-specific skills, including writing for and engaging communities online. Some examples of research-oriented projects include

- researching current practices and trends in digital media,
- strategizing with social media content,
- researching and writing for grants, or
- conducting a rhetorical media analysis.

Chapter 4 describes a variety of research-based media analysis projects. When community partners build capacity with emerging media platforms and literacies, they can make a significant impact with modest resources—becoming more effective in their work and in their reach as they challenge injustices and systemic inequalities. Learning to leverage media platforms to advocate for and with local community organizations provides students a meaningful way to engage in community-building approaches that pursue social justice.

The Beautiful Social Research Collaborative

In the spring of 2010, during my first year as a tenure-track faculty member, I created a social media course for the new communication studies program at my institution, Saint Joseph's University in Philadelphia, Pennsylvania. While speaking to an acquaintance who worked at the YMCA (Young Men's Christian Association), I mentioned that the course focused on studying the social web and how it could be used as a platform to manifest ethical action and civic engagement. Immediately, he asked if the students in the course would help him to understand how to use Facebook to support the message of the YMCA to a younger demographic. He said he didn't grasp the value of social media but knew he had to understand it to reach the nonprofit's audience. When I brought this request back to the students, the response was enthusiastic. Students stayed after class, discussing how they could collaborate with the YMCA to understand how social media could work with the organization in furthering its mission "to develop a healthy body, mind, and spirit." Having a full semester together to put theory into practice, students said that they wanted to ally with people and organizations who were trying to make a positive change in the world.

Motivated by the beautiful, social aspect of working side-by-side with partners who were driven to make transformative change, we embarked that day on a class project to understand how local nonprofits and cause-based organizations can harness the power of the social web to connect with their audiences and achieve their goals. That semester we took a team-based approach to working with the YMCA and the Rotary Club on social media strategies for Facebook and Twitter. We learned that the success of a community project takes everyone working together, researching, writing, editing, designing, and presenting. For detailed descriptions of collaborative team-based work, see Appendix B: Roles on Teams.

That semester, while learning (sometimes the hard way) about working with community partners, we began to see possibilities for the course project that could last long after the semester officially ended. To help control some of the logistical chaos involved with community-engaged research, I asked, what if there were a system to connect student media projects with organizations that wanted to grow and pursue research together? In response to that question, I founded the Beautiful Social Research Collaborative, a community-engaged writing program. In the Beautiful Social Research Collaborative (or B: Social as students call it), students in upper-level courses lead media-rich research projects with local nonprofit and community-based organizations. Through strategic partnerships, organizations receive support (at no cost) on an issue they identify while students gain valuable experience putting theory into practice. Collaboration is the key to successful partnerships—"derived from the Latin cum (with) and laborare (to work), collaboration means the act of working alongside someone to achieve something" (Manzini, 2015, p. 83). Collaborative organizations "are social groups emerging in highly connected environments. Their members choose to collaborate to achieve specific results, and in doing so, they create social, economic, and environmental benefits" (Manzini, 2015, p. 83). I viewed the Beautiful Social Research Collaborative not only as a creative community of people working together but also as a system. I realized this system could be designed intentionally as a writing program that conducted useful research in communities. I turned to Grabill's (2010) work on outreach research in which he noted, "To think of writing programs as infrastructure for outreach and research is, in my view, to place writing programs in a new category within taxonomies of university programs" (p. 21).

Encouraged by the idea that "what a writing program does, therefore, helps determine what it is" (Grabill, 2010, p. 15), I began talking about and framing the collaborative, not as a simple class project but as a complex network (or institution, even) with multiple stakeholders, strategies, visions, beliefs, and even policies centered around our central ideas. Grabill (2010) has claimed that "entities that do high-quality outreach research are rare because they lack the ethos, the personnel, the opportunity, or the disciplinary and methodological freedom to inquire in these ways" (p. 27). I knew if I wanted to achieve the high-quality work that we were capable of in Greater Philadelphia, I had to embrace the "methodological freedom" that comes with starting a new kind of writing program at my institution. Grabill (2007) ended his book *Writing Community Change: Designing Technologies for Citizen Action* by stating, "Writing programs can be part of the very infrastructure that supports communities writing for change" (p. 124). I contemplated this ending as a possibility, as an experiment in writing program design.

Twelve years later, the program is at the center of a thriving department, one of the largest in the college of arts and sciences at my institution. When the Beautiful Social Research Collaborative is ready to set up new partnerships for the upcoming semester, we put out a public call through social media channels to request proposals from interested organizations (see Appendix C: Locating Community Partners for more details). We collaborate with various nonprofit and community-based organizations via a writing-intensive upper-division course for third- and fourth-year undergraduate students in our communication and media studies department. Students in the Beautiful Social Research Collaborative pursue answers to current community-driven questions regarding media practices. This community-engaged writing program was founded on the premise that nonprofit and community-based organizations rely on strategic communication to create social change. The study of media (both new and old) can contribute to designing products for knowledge making and can support communities in communicating more effectively and persuasively.

The Beautiful Social Research Collaborative is a model of community-engaged writing that transforms classroom learning and ultimately teaches students how to become agents of social change by working alongside partners to tackle community-identified challenges. Students in this writing program have led with communities more than one hundred research projects free of charge in new media and social web consultancy, training, professional writing, social media management, online survey design, web design, and web-based video. In its first twelve years, we have

- advocated for people without housing and jobs, people who are disabled, who have been abused, who have a mental illness, who have a disease, who are injured, and who are hungry;
- built capacity within institutions to promote literacy, provide counseling, support job training, develop clean energy, and advocate child welfare;
- supported projects on behalf of prisoners seeking rehabilitation, veterans healing from combat-related disabilities, formerly incarcerated people navigating reentry, and neglected and abused children;
- campaigned to fund research to fight disease and provide medical services for cancer, diabetes, celiac disease, spinal cord injuries, heart disease, and Multiple Sclerosis;
- provided resources for local organizations to ensure safe shelter, medical care, clothing, school supplies, and healthy food to at-risk women and children;
- launched initiatives with community partners to bring books, toys, musical instruments, sports, urban parks, mindfulness training, after-school programs, technology, and summer camp into the lives of inner-city youth;
- researched emerging communication technologies to promote music, art, sculpture, nature, science, community theater, cross-cultural interaction, and peace and humanitarian initiatives;
- hosted public events to promote restorative justice, women's leadership, social entrepreneurship, and memorial fundraisers; and
- collaborated with over 100 community partners both locally in Greater Philadelphia and globally in Ethiopia, Kenya, Sierra Leone, South Sudan, The Gambia, Haiti, the United Kingdom, and throughout South America.

To view a complete list, please visit https://www.beautifulsocial.org/partners.

The Beautiful Social Research Collaborative embodies a long-standing commitment to working with community organizations to carry out projects that advance and share knowledge about media and communication that have real-world impact. The driving force behind this collaborative is not just to achieve measurable impact or results on any given project (rewarding in its own right) but also to create mutually beneficial relationships with allies who are committed to creating just and equitable futures. This includes working with local organizations regarding their media and communication practices and other academic partners who wish to enact a culture of change making and community building at their respective institutions.

Case Study: Life After Life

This section offers a community partner project case study and illustrates our equity-based approach to writing and designing with communities. It highlights the situated local action and decision-making process that guides our work but that is often invisible from view.

In the fall semester of 2019, a student team at the Beautiful Social Research Collaborative partnered with the newly formed community-based organization Life After Life, which sought to develop a website to increase its digital presence. Life After Life is a community of formerly incarcerated men and women who were sentenced to a term of life in prison without the possibility of parole for involvement in a homicide as children. They had their sentences reduced due to the landmark Miller v. Alabama decision of 2012, in which the United States Supreme Court deemed mandatory life-without-parole sentences unconstitutional for defendants under eighteen. As an organization comprised of people directly affected by the Supreme Court decision, Life After Life wanted to build a website to support other life-sentenced children and returning citizens transition into society after spending decades in prison.

One of the most critical aspects of the community writing program is our face-to-face meetings with community partners. We met with Life After Life throughout the semester in a communications classroom on campus because the organization does not currently have a common meeting location. The classroom provided a flexible space with moveable tables and chairs and access to laptops and media equipment, including a screen and data projector, for the group's meetings and training sessions. For more insight and logistics into the meeting process, see Appendix D: Meeting With Community Partners.

Building Empathy

In the Beautiful Social Research Collaborative, we create a research context where positionality, power, and privilege are actively considered in order to build empathy. In the first week of class, we begin building toward empathy with an activity on positionality and oppression. This activity includes looking at how we are positioned (by ourselves, by others, by particular discourse communities) in relation to multiple, relational social processes of difference (gender, class, race, ethnicity, age, education, ability, religion, nationality, sexuality) (details about this activity are in Appendix A: Positionality Activity). Doing this work means taking a critical look at how we are each positioned differently in hierarchies of power and privilege. This early work leads us into discussions about the role of positionality in the context of research ethics—especially how power dynamics flow through the research process and why it's our work to mindfully attend to our role in the contextual power interplay of the research process with community partners.

For this project, student group members needed to learn more about the history of juvenile incarceration and recent changes to the law to become better allies with members of Life After Life. In a blog post for the Juvenile Law Center, one of the organization's founders, Aaron Abd'Allah Lateef Phillips (2018), wrote that "there are others, like myself, who are full of promise and potential but void of opportunities to fully integrate into society" (para. 12). Throughout our conversations with Life After Life, and in-class reflections, some student group members were humbled to learn that their assumptions about formerly incarcerated people were misinformed. As one student admitted, "So often, people make the assumption that people who have been incarcerated have an awakening moment while in prison that ultimately empowers them to change their life around. I was one of those people." Instead, students learned that Life After Life argues that the potential for good was always there inside those who have been incarcerated and did not arise from time spent in the prison system, nor was it nurtured or protected in the environments in which those who became incarcerated grew up.

In getting to know this community group, it was apparent that empathy isn't always enough. We cannot always access empathy with our partners to the extent that we can truly understand their experiences and share their feelings. A few moments of insight cannot substitute for lived experience. Humility can serve us well in accessing compassion and empathy when working with our community partners. We need to hold courageous conversations, be vulnerable, experience discomfort, admit mistakes and wrong assumptions, acknowledge that we don't know. These are all ways of loosening those traditional, hierarchical power structures found in many traditional service-learning and community-engaged partnerships. Reflections are a time to consider events from a deeper perspective to better understand ourselves and our community partners. When students in this group openly acknowledged that they had been wrong in their initial assumptions about Life After Life regarding the potential for good, they made some headway. Empathy-building and reflective practices pave the way for collaborative learning and power-sharing in community partnerships. See Appendix E: Facilitating Reflection for both group and individual practices.

Framing Inquiry

The design (or research) question frames inquiry around the community-identified goal and works to structure the project. When Life After Life initiated this project, its goal was to build a website to develop its digital presence. As we started to frame inquiry around this goal, we began to understand the organization's vision. Framing inquiry around the project was a collective, back-and-forth process that emerged from in-depth conversations around access to technology, as pictured in Figure 3.1. After an initial meeting with Life After Life, it was clear that the organization wanted a website that was a "one-stop-shop" featuring

- blog posts that showcased personal stories and biographies of the members,
- press mentions and highlights of the group's members,
- podcasts/audio stories that featured personal stories and biographies of the members, and
- videos that featured personal stories and biographies of the members.

Moreover, via its website and social media, Life After Life wanted to recruit new members, provide resources and opportunities to support formerly incarcerated individuals, and advocate for policy change within the judicial system. After these initial discussions and some class activities on framing inquiry, we arrived at a design question that specifically stated the focus of the project: How might we support formerly life-sentenced children and advocate for policy change through storytelling via a WordPress website?

Figure 3.1. Framing Inquiry with Life After Life

Co-Creating Knowledge

When engaging in methods of collaborative knowledge production in the Beautiful Social Research Collaborative, we place emphasis and value on community-based knowledge. When working with Life After Life, framing inquiry helped to establish some direction for the project and allowed us to co-develop insights, identify opportunities, and better understand the underlying vision of the project. It became clear Life After Life could accomplish many of its goals for the project by emphasizing and sharing their collective knowledge and experience. It was clear that life experience was a strength and the source of passion. We realized this experience could be harnessed for good to mentor others who were navigating reentry and to support child-advocacy organizations and initiatives. After conducting media activities in class that focused on the organization's purpose, mission, and vision, we met with Life After Life to develop a more explicit mission statement and "about page" content for their website. This was a lengthy conversation that ultimately resulted in a more concise statement that outlined the goals of the organization:

> We . . . endeavor to use our collective voice and unique perspectives as former life-sentenced children in order to:
>
> 1. Enlighten policy-makers, stakeholders and the general public about the adverse consequences of imposing extremely lengthy sentences upon youthful offenders.
>
> 2. Engage with media outlets in order to profile stories of transformation, healing and redemption.
>
> 3. Support other child-advocacy organizations (and initiatives) that are headed by and/or informed by the collective wisdom gained from formerly incarcerated persons.
>
> 4. Develop innovative youth outreach and at-risk teen intervention strategies using our collective experience, influence and mentoring capacity in order to curb the epidemic of violence, drug abuse and bullying that is rampant within many high schools across the Commonwealth of Pennsylvania—including restorative justice practices, community healing & restoration. (Life After Life, n.d., para. 2)

It can be beneficial to newly formed organizations to hold these kinds of mission-building conversations. While it is not necessarily our role to direct or lead the conversation, we can be engaged listeners and ask guiding questions to better hone in on the organization's mission and purpose as well as structure the conversation in a productive manner, especially when there are a multitude of voices and ideas at the table and meeting time is limited.

Re-searching

Research is refined by investigating methods that best inform the research or design question. With our design question in hand, we began to conduct research to create the website prototype for Life After Life. The student team conducted a comparative media analysis that examined mentor accounts to help our partner explore potential strategies and possibilities for the website (this analysis is described in the next chapter). The group collected and annotated a list of comparable websites with mission statements similar to Life After Life's that they shared in a presentation. The mentor accounts included

- The Innocence Project—a nonprofit organization dedicated to freeing innocent people who remain incarcerated and to providing support and reform around unjust imprisonment,
- DreamCorps Justice—a bipartisan organization that works to reduce crime and incarceration across all 50 states, and
- *The Incarcerated Children's Advocacy Network (ICAN)*—a group of formerly incarcerated adults who create positive change in their communities.

With our analysis of the tactics and effectiveness of the various mentor accounts, Life After Life was better able to articulate what they wanted from its own website, how it could be structured, and what it could look like. It also became more evident that the organization wanted a platform on which it could tell personal stories. Not everyone in the group, however, was comfortable with writing alphabetic text. We needed to make sure that podcasts and video could be incorporated into the site at a later date.

Composing and Recomposing

In composing and recomposing, we bring ideas to life through tangible means to create a draft or prototype. Midway through the semester, the B: Social team was ready to create a website prototype for Life After Life. A design persona activity served to guide the process of production. Some of the student team members had previously taken a course called "web design and development," a required course in our communication and media studies department. This web design course serves as an introduction to the theory and practice of web design. Students learn about web technologies and standards, responsive design, accessibility, and mobile technologies. They also code a multi-page portfolio website in HTML5. This background knowledge was useful to team members as they built the site. The team worked with Life After Life to purchase the domain name and set up the initial site. They used the fully hosted version of WordPress, WordPress.com, for ease of use and installation, and the prototype could be transferred to a self-hosted site later if desired.

The B: Social team chose a theme that worked with both WordPress.com and the self-hosted version of WordPress, WordPress.org, in case Life After Life eventually decided to transfer over to WordPress.org, which would give the organization more flexibility in how the site looks and functions. The Balasana theme the team chose to create the front-end styling of the page featured a clean and minimalist design. The team felt that a black and white color scheme depicted reality and set the tone for the documentary storytelling that the site would eventually feature. As Darren R. Reid (2015) wrote of his choice to use black and white film in a documentary movie, "It was as if a lack of colour served to create a semi-blank canvas onto which an audience could project emotion or sentiment" (para. 6). Students explained that the choice of a limited color palette would highlight Life After Life's stories and not overwhelm the site with unnecessary ornament.

Testing and Revision

We gather feedback about the prototype in the testing and revision phase and synthesize that feedback into insights for further refinement. When the website prototype was nearing completion, we met with Life After Life for site feedback and provided some training with the WordPress interface. The B: Social team walked the members of the organization through the existing pages, including the home page, about page, blog page, and contact page. The group discussed the goals of ultimately posting blog posts, press mentions, podcasts, videos, and biographies of the individuals involved. We also spent some time talking about how the "voice" of the organization was portrayed via the site and how Life After Life could connect with its audience by developing its collective voice. Since Life After Life wanted to reach different audiences and stakeholders via the site, the group wanted to create a cohesive voice across the board. After the discussion, everyone agreed that the site's voice needed to be serious (but not intimidating) while also friendly and inviting (but not too casual).

In the media training session that followed, B: Social worked with some of the members of Life After Life. In a hands-on demonstration, members learned the basics of navigating WordPress, including logging in, adding and editing media, and creating new pages and posts. The members of Life After Life were beginners to blogging and using digital media in general. The team used resources such as the website Nonprofit WP—The Start-to-Finish WordPress Guide for Nonprofits (https://nonprofitwp.org/) to talk through with Life After Life the process of content creation. We ended the feedback and training session to discuss how Life After Life would like our community-university partnership to move forward. Members of Life After Life talked about how they had been inspired by the film *It's a Hard Truth Ain't It*. They explained that the documentary is directed by thirteen incarcerated men and gives the audience an intimate look at their lives. In this film, the subjects interview each other and talk about their past and where they are now. Life After Life expressed great interest in creating a similar kind of film with an interview-in-the-round format. They also proposed an entirely different training workshop to learn how to use social media for advocacy work. We made a plan to continue working with Life After Life on the interview-in-the-round video project the next year. Due to the COVID-19 pandemic, this project was postponed.

Evaluating Capacity

Evaluating how the community has built capacity through the project is a shared endeavor between community and university partners. This project built capacity for Life After Life by developing a mission statement and creating a website. With these tools, the organization was better able to connect to a variety of stakeholders about its mission. A media training session also built capacity around basic blogging skills and connecting to the audience. Creating this website was the first step in a much larger project that speaks to developing a generative community-university relationship that spans multiple semesters. Students involved with Life After Life were engaged and profoundly impacted through the work. Three of the students involved in the project went on to take leadership roles within the Beautiful Social Research Collaborative as course mentors or fellows (students who lead group projects).

Phillips, the Life After Life founder who participated in this case study, responded to an evaluation survey at the end of the semester. He expressed that he had "nothing but the highest forms of commendation for the students who went above and beyond in their dedication to elevating the visibility and storytelling of former life-sentenced children." He said that the project "met their expectations and that the collaboration went extremely well." He indicated that he looked forward to continuing the partnership and "conducting in-person interviews, recording of a round-table discussion, and creation of b-roll for our video-based web content." Although the project was deemed successful in many ways, the project also had its challenges. Although the website is technically ready for the group's use, it has not been utilized by members of Life After Life (as of this writing). Clearly, sharing stories is not as simple as having a website. This brings to question issues around project sustainability. It is possible that more guidance and technology training is needed, including training for login and posting procedures, since members of Life After Life are not familiar with the WordPress platform and creating posts for a blog. The group mentioned that they would like to collaborate on storytelling facilitation to capture their personal stories for the website. Due to the pandemic, we have not yet been able to resume our partnership and build upon the work we began. Having an expansive view of our partnership relationship (beyond the scope of the semester) means that we have the time and space to continue working with Life After Life.

In Summer 2020, Stacey Torrance, a community member of Life After Life, initiated an off-shoot project with B: Social. In the 2021–22 academic year we collaborated with Torrance to launch the Free Mind Entrepreneur Network. This organization provides entrepreneurship resources for formerly incarcerated individuals. We worked with Torrance to create the logo, social media accounts, and website for the organization. In a short amount of time, the former CEO of the NAACP Real Estate Division and Philadelphia's District Attorney has expressed interest in joining the organization's efforts to reduce recidivism, promote entrepreneurship, and showcase racial inequities in the prison system. By framing our research as a long-term process that builds community, we can work toward more profound, more sustainable long-term commitments.

Chapter 4. How Might We Develop Our Students' Skills in Writing and Rhetoric via Emerging Media While Working With Our Community Partners to Build Capacity?

Chapter 4 walks through a series of media analysis projects that build capacity in the use of emerging media. Through media analysis, students learn to leverage media platforms strategically to advocate with and for community organizations. Students take an active role in working with rhetoric, writing, and media studies theories as they conduct research with communities and produce new knowledge that will benefit their partners. Media analysis creates opportunities to relate to, participate in, and apply course material to real-world needs. Emphasizing active knowledge construction over the passive transmission of information, students take ownership of the complex concepts they encounter and can transfer that knowledge to school, workplace, and community contexts. Media analysis helps writing students frame themselves as participants within a research community. It also asks students to examine and participate in timely methodological issues with tools pertinent to current scholarship in the disciplines of writing studies, rhetoric, new media, communications, and the field of engaged scholarship.

Community Partner Report Components

The media analysis projects described in this chapter can be edited and combined into a more extensive community partner report. It is not necessary to complete all of the media analysis projects for the report. The report can be tailored to the specifications of the community partner and presented near the end of the semester. The media analysis projects that might be used in the report are as follows:

- **Design question analysis**—Community-engaged projects are based on a community-driven desire to build capacity or create change. This activity guides both students and partners in developing the design question to frame inquiry around a community-identified goal.
- **Social media analysis**—Learning to leverage social media platforms to advocate for and with local community organizations provides students a meaningful way to engage in the public work of composition. In this analysis, groups objectively observe and describe the state of their community partner's social media platforms.

- **Comparative media analysis**—Drawing from the section "Nonprofit Examples of Excellence" in *Social Media for Social Good: A How-To Guide for Nonprofits* (Mansfield, 2011), students create a list of social media examples that are tailored to the organization's needs. By locating three comparable social media accounts, groups explore potential media strategies and possibilities for community partners to employ.
- **Golden circle analysis**—Sometimes called "knowing your why," (Sinek, 2011, p. 50) the golden circle is an effective tactic to get a bird's eye view of an organization; as popularized by brand strategist Sinek (2011), the golden circle can be used to help map an organization's why, how, and what.
- **Social object rhetorical analysis**—Drawing from contemporary social theorists Cetina (1997, 2001, 2007) and Engeström (2005), this analysis invites students to examine how communities connect through shared objects and helps students consider how the concept of social objects can be applied to their community partner's communication strategy.
- **Organizational storytelling**—Storytelling is a way for an organization to humanize itself. This analysis activity guides students in numerous ways to tell stories that elicit a strong sense of pathos while engaging deeply with the organization's audience on a personal level.

Each project is described in more detail in the next sections. At the end of the semester, students revise and edit their media analyses and combine all that is useful into one report that they present to their community partners at a meeting or event. The community partner report offers our partners new approaches to engaging their audiences via emerging media.

Design Question Analysis

An analysis of the design question, also called the research question, frames inquiry around a community-identified goal and works to structure the project. The design question analysis can be conducted during the first meeting with the community partner. Before the first meeting, community partners can identify an area of interest or issue to investigate. (For more about the process of locating partners, please see Appendix C: Locating Community Partners.) Then, at the first meeting with community partners, we can begin by asking the community partners to tell us about their organization at large, including its origins. We can continue the conversation by asking our partners to explain the research issue they have identified and a little about what is at stake for them. Once the primary issue becomes more evident, we can develop a design question that guides our research for that issue.

One way to do this is to put the issue into a question format. This may take a few attempts to get right. A design question, for our purposes, is a clear statement about a phenomenon of interest, a condition to be improved upon, an issue to be explored, or a question that exists in theory or practice for the partner's field or organization. Since our partnerships are based on a community-driven desire to build capacity or to create change, this question should originate from the community partner. We can then work with them to refine the question. There are many kinds of questions we can develop, such as the following:

- **"What is"** questions describe a phenomenon, issue, or behavior and refer to what it currently looks like (or looked like in the past).
  - **Example** (*mapping relevant content*): What is an editorial calendar, and how can it be used as a tool to identify the best days of the year to connect with our audience about our mission? This type of project could include research on best practices and the development of a scheduling calendar to keep the organization on track with posting timely and relevant content to social media channels.
- **"What works"** questions seek to find evidence for the effectiveness of particular strategies.
  - Example (*building trust with an influencer*): How can we increase trust and credibility for our nonprofit by cultivating a relationship with a media influencer? This project could include examining what happens when the nonprofit partners with an influencer (someone who can persuade others to support the nonprofit's programs) and then tracking audience engagement over a certain number of weeks.
- **"What if"** questions look at visions of what could be done and explore new strategies.
  - Example (*strategizing with video*): What if we boost our fundraising efforts through the use of video via a YouTube channel? This project could include research about how organizations can invest in video and strategy development and employ video as an ongoing means of communication for social good (not merely as a one-off campaign).

Design research with community partners involves studying how something works. Sometimes the initial questions are too vague or broad in context. Using a question format, both parties can determine if the research needs to be refined or narrowed down in order to be useful to the partner. An initial research question does not need to state how to do something, offer a vague or broad proposition, or present a value question. We do not need to indicate how we will work together to answer this question at this point—we only need a clear statement about what the research project encompasses. Once a generative research question is agreed upon by all parties (community partners and student groups), the research question can then be further refined and narrowed to create a feasible project and can work toward meaningful impact for the community partner.

To better understand the intent behind the project, we can also ask our community partners to tell us more about the purpose behind this project. For example, the deeper meaning of the project might be to find out how to share knowledge effectively, how to connect to a community or demographic, how to reach potential donors, or how to promote a successful event. We can also use this time as an opportunity to discuss any background context about the project, including upcoming events or deadlines.

Lastly, we can ask the following: Who are the potential stakeholders or audiences for this project? Who benefits from this research/project? How many different kinds of stakeholders are there? (Usually, there are multiple stakeholders.) How do they each benefit?

We can wrap up this discussion focused on what, why, and who by reiterating the three takeaways from this session:

- What—Our research question is _____.
- Why—Our purpose for pursuing the project is _____.
- Who—Our potential audiences/stakeholders for this issue are _____.

Below are example responses from the Juvenile Justice Center that resulted from this question-based process during a past community partner project. The Juvenile Justice Center provides an array of services to youth and families who enter its program through the Philadelphia Family Court, the Philadelphia Department of Human Services, and Community Umbrella Agencies, agencies designated by the city of Philadelphia to provide case management services.

> Q: *What is the issue?*
>
> A: We have lost the funding we previously had to run the organization and are trying to obtain donations. We want to let people know about the different services we offer for youth and families who enter the Philadelphia Family Court system, the Department of Human Services, and Community Umbrella Agencies.
>
> Q: *What is the purpose of the project?*
>
> A: We want people to know about the services we offer and the impact we can have on the lives of the youth who go through our programs. Doing this may allow someone to find the Juvenile Justice Center and use it for all it offers. Others may find the Juvenile Justice Center and feel compassion for the stories we tell and the work we do through our foster care program, therefore deeming it a worthy cause for them to support us financially.
>
> Q: *What are some possible ideas for projects?*
>
> A: Developing a more robust online community through social media channels could be an idea. A video or video series that showcases the Juvenile Justice Center's services could help us reach our audience and potential donors.

Q: What are some of the foreseeable challenges?

A: One challenge we face in this project is our inability to photograph or video the children being served by the Juvenile Justice Center. We are not able to feature them without parental consent. Also, how can we draw people in to become donors while not making it seem like we are only asking for money? Also, how can we raise awareness so that children can benefit from the services of The Juvenile Justice Center?

Q: What is the project's Design Question?

A: How might we create a short video for The Juvenile Justice Center website that promotes conversation and encourages active members in the Philadelphia community to advocate on behalf of the Juvenile Justice Center?

By working through guiding questions together, the student group and the community partner can arrive at a project that meets the partner's vision. While this student group originally wanted to film multiple videos, they decided to focus on just one video highlighting the different services that the Juvenile Justice Center offers youth and families. The partner could use this video on the organization's website and social media channels. In a project evaluation, Jeanine Glasgow, Executive Director at the Juvenile Justice Center of Philadelphia, said, "The group did a great job capturing the goal of the project, that featured a video that provided an overview of the programs we provide for families. I wish we had a few students for an entire semester to be on site."

Social Media Analysis

Learning to leverage social media platforms to advocate with and for local community organizations provides students a meaningful way to engage in the public work of composition. Media scholar Howard Rheingold (2007) proposed,

By showing students how to use web-based tools and channels to inform the public, advocate positions, contest claims, and organize action around issues that they truly care about, participatory media education can draw them into positive early experiences with citizenship that could influence their civic behavior throughout their lives. (p. 102)

Bridgette Wessels (2018) similarly argued, "The development of a more networked organisation of civic life and the increased use of social media to raise awareness, connect and mobilise people around civic issues has ushered in a communicative civic-ness" (p. 3). As these scholars have noted, working with social media can be a generative and motivating way to develop students' writing, rhetorical, and civic participation skills. However, writing scholars David Dadurka and Stacey Pigg (2011) acknowledged that

> we have only begun to show how social media can play a dramatic role in academic contexts and what value they hold for teaching students how to acquire literacies that will benefit their professional and civic lives in college and beyond. (p.17)

The assignment to complete a social media analysis can be an entry point into teaching students how to be critical of technology and how to apply analytical frameworks to that technology. While some students may feel comfortable using digital platforms in their work with communities, other students need detailed instruction to fully engage with the range of affordances involved in the application of digital tools. For example, some students do not necessarily know (or have not considered) what the terms "social web" or "social networks" technically denote, nor are they always able to articulate that these things are primarily designed "for user-generated content" (Manzini, 2015, p. 81) or for what Wessels (2018) called "the creation and sharing of information, ideas, and other forms of expression through digitally supported networks" (p. 2). While students most likely know how to use Facebook and Instagram for their personal use, they may not yet know how to apply social theories of engagement to these platforms. This activity helps foster understanding of how the social web's community-building power can be applied to cause-based organizations.

In the social media analysis activity, groups observe and describe the state of the community partner's social media platforms. The results of this activity can be included in the more extensive community partner report and lays the foundation for future media analysis. This social media analysis project gives both university and community partners an objective evaluation of "what is." The research reveals the current state of a partner's various social media platforms. Gaining a clear perspective on the partner's platforms helps locate opportunities to support the partner in connecting with its audience.

We begin this activity by examining each social media platform and taking detailed notes on each of the platforms in use by the partner—including the partner's Twitter, Facebook, and Instagram channels, among others. This is known as a social media audit and is used to consider the organization's metrics in order to "assess growth, opportunities and what can be done to improve . . . social presence" (Barnhart, 2020, para. 7). Students can examine each platform both qualitatively and quantitatively. We do not need access to analytics software or our community partner's login information to do this work; students can gather all the information needed for the analysis by closely observing their partner's social media channels and interactions. Students can record the data they collect from each platform in a spreadsheet or use a ready-made template from the Beautiful Social Research Collaborative. (The template is available at https://docs.google. com/spreadsheets/d/1LWyS5TIlhMXr9fIv4dFAZP6L6A-iUAUtYvnhm5Jo3ZA/ edit?usp=sharing. To use the template, students will need to make a copy or download it as an Excel spreadsheet.)

Once the audit is complete, students can then summarize their findings by using the following guiding questions focused on a few key areas:

- **Platform tactics**—Examine the number of followers for each platform. Is the same content being used on different platforms, or is the content tailored to each platform? How so? How frequent are the posts? On what days and times do the posts on each platform occur?
- **Content**—What is the conveyed message on each platform? What kind of information is shared on each platform? What types of posts are used—informational, promotional, relatable, or interactive (such as polls or a call-to-action)? What kinds of media (video, links, text, image, etc.) are shared? Is there a cohesive message across all platforms? What is it? Does the over-arching message differ between platforms? Which ones? How so?
- **Audience interactions**—Social media interaction is about building relationships. Relationships are not built in a single conversation or transaction. Instead, they are built over time. In *Storytelling in the Digital Age: A Guide for Nonprofits*, Julia Campbell (2017) asked, "When you post a photo, video, or link, does anyone respond? Or are there crickets? Engagement metrics are useful in figuring out what your community values and what types of stories resonate" (p. 171). What types of audience interactions do you see on each platform? Are all interactions directed to the organization, or does the audience ever speak to each other? What kinds of conversations do they have? How would you categorize them? How many different kinds of interactions are there? (How many replies? How many retweets?) What is the estimated ratio between "listening" (replies, retweets) posts vs. "talking" posts (posts in which the organization shares information about itself)?

When the audit sections (platform tactics, content, and audience interactions) have been thoroughly examined, students write up the findings in a concise, organized report. The goals are to arrive at a clear awareness of how our community partners are currently using social media platforms and to identify opportunities for future action. This activity is not overly concerned with value judgments, suggestions for new practices, or ideas for the organization—those will come later. The goal here is simply to articulate, in an impartial way, what is happening on the partner's platforms. If a student group is implementing a social media change or campaign project during the semester, it is recommended that they use this analysis tool to track or demonstrate changes over time (such as weekly) to analyze engagement. This analysis can be used for any platform, including Facebook, Instagram, Twitter, blogs, YouTube, and others.

Here are some tips for students to use in writing the analysis:

- Give some thought to the organization of the analysis.
- Write in clear, concise, complete sentences.
- Use neutral/objective/descriptive language rather than subjective/judgmental language.
- Include and caption screenshots or images where applicable.
- Use statistics and data visualizations to illustrate points.

Comparative Media Analysis

When completing the comparative media analysis, students locate three or more mentor accounts and explore potential media strategies and possibilities for community partners to employ. This research allows student groups to better identify with community partners by locating mentor accounts or exemplary accounts. In *Rewriting Partnerships: Community Perspectives on Community-Based Learning*, Shah (2020) reported that her interviewee Sarah Gonzales advised that students could ask, "What are three good websites we should look at that show work similar to yours?" (p. 79). By creating a resource of at least three comparable accounts, students can better understand the discourses of a particular nonprofit field and learn more about the context of the community partner's organization, leading to a more productive project and relationship.

Comparative media analyses can also be employed to provide valuable tactics used by other successful organizations. Drawing from the section "Nonprofit Examples of Excellence" in *Social Media for Social Good: A How-To Guide for Nonprofits* by Mansfield (2011), students can create a list of exemplary accounts and content. Mansfield suggested creating lists for concrete phenomena of interest, such as best nonprofit LinkedIn groups, best examples of "text to give" campaigns, and best use of nonprofit e-newsletters. The more specific and focused the lists of mentor accounts are, the more helpful they will be in producing examples and suggestions tailored to the organization's needs.

For example, in fall 2020, a student group worked with Chenoa Manor, a nonprofit animal sanctuary in Avondale, Pennsylvania. Chenoa Manor incorporates Buddhist ideals into the care of its animal residents and the education of visitors. When tropical storm Isaias destroyed some fencing on the sanctuary property in August 2020, Chenoa Manor had to halt its youth and educational programming due to safety risks. The nonprofit found itself in "desperate need" of fundraising to repair the downed fences. In their comparative media analysis, students researched three leading animal sanctuaries that have been effective at fundraising and connecting with their audiences about animal rights issues—The Kangaroo Sanctuary, Black Jaguar White Tiger Foundation, and Greenwood Wildlife Rehabilitation Center. In their analysis, the students examined each foundation's fundraising and audience engagement tactics in order to plan a successful fund-raising campaign with Chenoa Manor.

Once the media analysis is complete, students can present their findings to the community partner for further discussion. Not only can a comparative media analysis drive the next phase of research in a project, but community partners can also refer back to mentor accounts when they are in search of inspiration or ideas for effective strategies of engagement. This analysis asks three things:

- Who are the three best mentor organizations for this situation?
- What are they doing that is exemplary?
- Why are they effective? (What is the evidence?)

When selecting mentor accounts, it can be helpful to consider three to five organizations that are similar to the community partner and that use digital media effectively as it pertains to the research question. Usually, the community partner will already know who some of their competitors or inspiration are. Students can take these suggestions into account when choosing the mentor accounts. Groups can also determine the mentor accounts by finding them mentioned in books, articles, case studies, online sources, hashtag searches, and active social media accounts. How did the group choose the top organizations (via case studies, hashtag search, direct competitors, media influencers, followers, word-of-mouth, etc.)? Students can discuss which methods were used to select the mentor accounts.

In writing the analysis, it can be helpful to organize it into sections that focus on three areas:

- **Strategy**—In this section, students discuss each mentor account, one at a time. How is this account demonstrating the phenomenon of interest (such as innovation or audience engagement)? What, specifically, does the account do? How is it doing it? (Students can include screenshots or images to illustrate claims, if necessary.)
- **Effectiveness**—Why are these practices effective? According to whom? What theory was used to define effectiveness? What is the evidence? Students can demonstrate an argument or cite sources from the course readings and use evidence to back up claims.
- **Summary**—Students can summarize their initial thoughts about how the community partner could benefit or borrow from some of these strategies and practices. What are the three main takeaways that might benefit the community partner? What tactics would be most beneficial to them as they move forward?

Golden Circle Analysis

The golden circle, or "knowing your why," is an effective tactic to get a bird's eye view of the community partner organization. According to Sinek (2011), the golden circle helps to visually map an organization's why, how, and what. In examining how inspiring leaders communicate, he claimed, "Every company knows what they do. Some companies know how they do it. Few companies know *why* they do it" (Sinek, 2011, p. 1). According to him, inspiring leaders work from the inside-out, starting with (a) the why, followed by (b) the how, and finally (c) the what.

Most organizations have a mission statement that is relatively easy to find. However, does that mission statement align to the organization's why, how, and what? Some organizations are quite clear about all three. Others focus most of their attention on the "what" to the extent that they neglect to refine their purpose—their reason for being there in the first place. When researching with a community partner, we need to deeply understand their "why"—their *raison d'etre*. We can discover this by asking the following questions:

- Why is there a need for this organization to do this work (locally, historically, culturally)?
- Why do people want or need this organization's content, product, or service?
- Why do people care?
- Why does the organization's content, product, or service benefit others?

Sinek (2017) has also claimed, "When a company has a strong WHY, it inspires trust and loyalty in its customers, clients, employees, and supporters, all of whom will cheer you on in your cause" (p. 118). For example, campaign contributors want to hear where the fundraised money is going. But first, they want to know *why* they need to donate money in the first place. Why should they be a part of this cause or movement? Why is this going to change lives? Justin Rosenstein and Katie De Carlo (n.d.), writing on behalf of Asana, a work management platform, claimed that "without an answer to the question 'why,' it's difficult to know which feature to develop, what markets to first enter, how employees should collaborate with one another, or how to make the millions of micro-choices required to build an organization" (para. 5). Putting the cause front and center creates a road map for further action. When working with community partners, we must be clear about the beliefs and values that drive them. For example, we worked with Young and Involved Philadelphia to rewrite their mission statement so that it aligned with their "why." After much drafting, we arrived at a clear and concise mission statement that described the motivation behind their cause "to promote active citizenship and emerging leadership among young Philadelphians" (Bojar, 2016, p. 87). The golden circle analysis assignment asks student groups to answer the following questions from the perspective of their community partner:

- **The why**—Why do we do what we do? What is the purpose, cause, belief, or idea that drives or inspires us? What difference do we want to make in the world?
- **The how**—How do we do our work? What methods do we employ? What actions set us apart from others?

- **The what**—What is our function? What content, product, or service do we offer the world?

Additionally, it is important to determine if everyone agrees on what the various components are. It often takes a couple of tries to create an accurate road map. Conducting a golden circle analysis for our partner Birchrun Hills Farm helped the organization understand the strong family values and traditions behind its small dairy farm. Since only some of this information was accessible via the web, students needed to learn more about the community-based organization through an interview-based discussion. In that interview, they gained a clearer understanding of Birchrun Hills Farm's mission and vision. Their findings included the following:

- **The why**—We believe farm-raised food makes communities stronger and more sustainable.
- **The how** We use traditional methods to operate a small dairy farm with a herd of 80 Holstein cows, grow crops, and run a community-based creamery and cheese aging facility.
- **The what**—We produce farm-to-table award-winning raw milk cheeses.

After determining these answers, we drew a why/how/what diagram. A why/how/what diagram is drawn as three concentric rings with the "why" in the center, the "how" in the middle, and the "what" on the periphery, as displayed in Figure 4.1. Students can draw and label their golden circle illustrations on a white board to share with the class. Sometimes after a discussion, groups find that they need to revise their circles or switch the position of the partner's "how" and "what." Groups can then use design software to create a visualization of the golden circle that can be included in the analysis report.

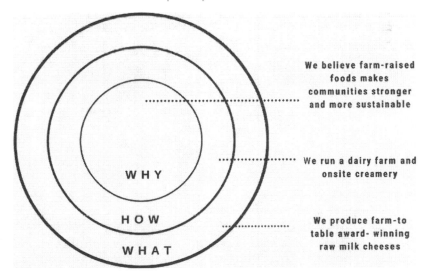

Figure 4.1. Birchrun Hills Farm Golden Circle

When we write up the golden circle analysis summary, we discuss the partner's mission and its relation to their golden circle (i.e., their why, how, and what). Community partners might not be aware of Sinek's (2011) golden circle, so students will need to keep the audience in mind and explain the concept in their own words.

Social Object Analysis

To understand what makes an engaging social web experience, we can ask what makes the "social web" social in the first place. The social web is defined by how people connect and interact with one another—for example, via social networking sites such as Facebook, YouTube, Twitter, and Instagram. Each social networking site features one or more social objects. In this activity, we will examine social objects—what they are, what they do, what they ask users to do, and how they bring people together. Looking at the nature of social objects gives us a way to write and design for a more engaging social web experience.

Connecting Through Shared Objects

As a general rule, a social network portrays connections or relationships between people. It usually shows people making connections with other people, building networks with each other, and engaging people within online communities. However, some contemporary social theorists and practitioners claim that something vital is missing from this picture—the reason why people are connected in the first place—the objects themselves. Drawing from contemporary social theorists Cetina (1997, 2001, 2007) and Engeström (2005), we can look at how people connect through shared objects. As Cetina (2007) has noted, social objects "mediate ties between humans" (p. 371). The argument here is that the object is the thing that links people together.

A classic example is a "water cooler conversation," a conversation that occurs near a tangible object around which people meet and connect at the workplace. Another social object is coffee. People have been meeting "for coffee" since 1475, when the first coffeehouse opened in Constantinople. The social, according to some social theorists, exists in *the way* things are connected. On the web, social objects abound. People go to Instagram to share images, people go to YouTube and Vimeo to share videos, and people go to Facebook and Twitter to share links and status updates. As a result, social networks consist of people connected by these shared objects (in these cases, the social objects are the images, the videos, and the updates). Engeström (2005) has explained that "social networks consist of people who are connected by a shared object" (para. 3). These objects have rhetorical agency, meaning they exist to persuade users to perform actions. When a site or service is designed around shared objects, it will help to facilitate a shared experience for the user.

Object-Oriented Practice

When it comes to object-oriented practice, practice is not about rule-based routines, literacy, or even skills. Practice, according to Cetina (2001), is understood in terms of a "'relational dynamics' that links subjects and objects" (as cited in Schatzki, 2001, p. 13). In other words, practice is the performance of an activity with, through, or by an object. When we write and design for the social web, it can be helpful to understand our audience's object-oriented practices within specific social media sites.

When people are using the social web, they don't technically interact with other "people." Instead, people's interactions are mediated through a site's social objects. For example, on Flickr, a photo-sharing site that came on the scene years before Instagram, the primary social object is the photograph, and members comment, reply, rate, and converse around photos. On Flickr and other social networks, objects often are nested within one another. Take, for example, the 365 days group on Flickr, which in itself contains millions of photographs. Here, people connect around a particular kind of photograph—the self-portrait or selfie. Nested subgroups exist for people who like to connect through portraits in bathrooms, or portraits on public transportation, or portraits just in silhouette, or portraits of hair.

The effectiveness of a social network depends on the effectiveness of its nodes—its hubs of convergence. Networks depend on their nodes. Nodes are indicated where several people or things come together from different directions to meet. In the Flickr example, nodes are found both in the image and in the textual comments. Nodes are also present in the larger community itself, which revolves around themes and variations of self-representation. Other nodes reflect people connecting on technical issues, such as Photoshop effects or camera equipment. Examining nodes, or points of convergence, helps bring to light what is important to community members. That is why Flickr (the company), continually evolves by examining points of connection, such as tagging, favoriting, and group pools of photographs, to reflect what its users have deemed important, even among its now over two million groups. Here are some equivalencies to remember: *object-oriented design = better user interaction = better engaged community*. To summarize:

- People interact with objects
- Objects are often nested
- Effectiveness depends on nodes—its hubs of convergence
- Nodes reflect what members value

String Theory Experiment Activity

This activity puts theory into practice. The concept of social objects and relational practices can be very abstract. To make the concepts more concrete, in my classes, I introduce this short, hands-on activity. My reading of Clara Shih's (2011) *The Facebook Era* inspired this activity; I adapted Shih's description of the reciprocity ring into an experiment with social objects. Shih's reciprocity ring builds from Mark S. Granovetter's (1973) well-known theory of the strength of weak ties within social networks. In Granovotter's research, he questioned the idea that the amount of overlap in two people's social networks corresponds directly with the strength of their relationship. Instead, he theorized about the power of weak ties. According to Granovetter (1973), an "emphasis on weak ties lends itself to a discussion of relations between groups and to an analysis of segments of social structure not easily defined in terms of primary groups" (p. 1360). The hands-on activity I developed demonstrates how a social object, in this case, a "status request," brings people together, as pictured in Figure 4.2.

Figure 4.2. Students at the whiteboard conducting the string theory experiment.

The steps in this activity are as follows:

1. Participants write their names and a tangible "status request" on sticky notes. Some examples of tangible status requests include asking for an umbrella, a ride home, a snack, a babysitting job, a futon, or an internship.
2. Participants place their sticky notes in a circle on a whiteboard or a table.
3. Participants survey the requests. When participants can contribute to requests, they write their names and how they can help on a new sticky note. Participants place their contribution notes below the original requests.
4. Participants then connect (with string) the status requests that have received responses to the people who offered contributions. The strings, in this case, show points of connection between the object (status request) and the people who offered a helpful contribution. Strings (or ties) go from the inner ring where students first posted their request to the various people from whom they received contributions.

This activity makes visible how objects themselves can be social; it demonstrates how objects facilitate the concept of sociality. It also allows us to physically observe specific social phenomena, including the amount of "overlap" within the activity and which objects are the most "social" by connecting the most people. This exercise makes visible how the social object, here the status request, mediates ties between people. People are not interacting directly with other people in this exercise. People interact with the social objects, the status requests. This activity helps students understand that social objects are rhetorically persuasive. Social objects prompt participants to perform activities. These activities are relational in nature— the more interactive the social object, the more opportunities for connection.

Social networks are a combination of strong and weak ties. If we take a look at our connections through one of our social media accounts, such as Twitter, Instagram, or Facebook, chances are, not every one of our followers will be a close friend or relative. It is even possible that there are people in our network we have never physically met in real life. What percentage of people in your networks would you categorize as a strong tie vs. weak tie (or loose connection)? The number of our strong tie relationships does not expand very much. Our best friends, closest acquaintances, and family grow at a relatively slow pace. However, our loose connections, our weak ties, can expand at an accelerated pace as we make connections and add new people to our social circle. Weak ties create "ambient intimacy"—defined by Leisa Reichelt (2007) as "being able to keep in touch with people with a level of regularity of intimacy that you wouldn't usually have access to, because time and space conspire to make it impossible" (para. 3). Randi Zuckerburg, former director of marketing at Facebook has said, "What makes Facebook so powerful is that an individual can share content with his or her friends, who in turn share it with their friends—and in just a short time, a large number of people can come together around a common interest in a truly global conversation" (as cited in Plastrik, et. al., 2014, p. 28).

Relational Practice

Social objects are designed to make demands on their users. When it comes to social media, through social objects, users perform all kinds of actions—users post, comment, link, follow, and like, to name a few. These are relational practices. We think of relational practices as chains of activity made possible through interaction with the objects themselves. These practices are easy to spot, as they are often associated with verbs. Verbs can point the way to which relational practices are happening through social objects. On Facebook, we used to be "fans" of things. We would click a button and become a fan. However, a fan is a noun. *To like* is a transitive verb (because it has a direct object). In February 2009, Facebook turned on the like button, and user's likes, interests, and activities turned into social objects virtually overnight. What this means is that on Facebook, we can now associate with our "likes." We assemble around them. One day I had been a fan of the pinball page on Facebook. Then the next day, I was linked to *everyone* on Facebook who also had an interest in pinball. Suddenly, I was part of a community of practice. This could be the moment that Facebook started to take social object theory to heart; the company redesigned its platform to turn the act of liking into a social experience, a way to build communities of practice.

Successful platforms such as Facebook are continually encouraging sociality and building communities through the creation of knowledge cultures. Although these ideas have been circulating for quite some time, they are not particularly well-known or understood. In their article "Digital Social Objects: Getting a Grip on Interaction," Michael Rander and Dan Wellers (n.d.) observed how social object theory can give the user an advantage and noted,

> At a time when few companies even know what digital social objects are, companies can gain a significant competitive advantage simply by understanding how social objects work and how to use them strategically to help their customers coalesce into a community. (para. 11)

Many successful social enterprises take social object theory to heart, watching for what encourages sociality and experimenting with how to best facilitate it. Putting this theory into practice is one of the best ways to support our community partners as they build their online communities of practice.

Relational Practices Activity

When we write and design for the social web, it is important to understand users' relational practices within a specific social media platform. Mapping relational practices give us a way to gather evidence about why some social web services succeed while others don't, with success based on how effectively a site's social objects bring people together. In this case, the phenomenon of interest is object-oriented practice. We want to know how online communities come together, how they make knowledge, and how they attribute value through their interaction via a platform's social objects. To assess this, we might choose the microblogging site Twitter and look at its status updates as an object-oriented practice. Twitter (n.d.) has claimed that it aims to "use the positive power of Twitter to strengthen our communities through our platform, people, and profits" (Our Mission section). What makes Twitter powerful? *How* does it strengthen communities? People go to Twitter to answer the question "What's happening?"; consequently, the object-oriented practice, in the case of Twitter, revolves around the status update.

To map the relational practices used on social media networks, students can complete the following steps:

1. Choose a social object (such as a status update) on a specific social media site (such as Twitter, Facebook, or Instagram).

2. Attend to the practices associated with the object. What actions do users perform with or through the object? What does the object persuade users to do? Create a list of verbs associated with the object on the site. For example, here are some practices that occur through the status update on Twitter:

   o   People tweet.
   o   People retweet.
   o   People tag and hashtag.
   o   People link.
   o   People reply.
   o   People mention.
   o   People favorite.

3. Label the practices and sub-practices associated with the object, as illustrated in Figure 4.3.

   o   Sub-practices:
       ▪   People link to photos
       ▪   People link to websites
       ▪   People link to videos

4. Continue labeling practices and sub-practices of all social objects on the site.

5. Discuss, based on the findings, how successful the individual objects are at bringing people. How does the audience construct knowledge, meaning, and attribute value through these practices? How could more interaction be encouraged? Are there missed opportunities for connection? How could a stronger community of practice be facilitated through the platform's social objects?

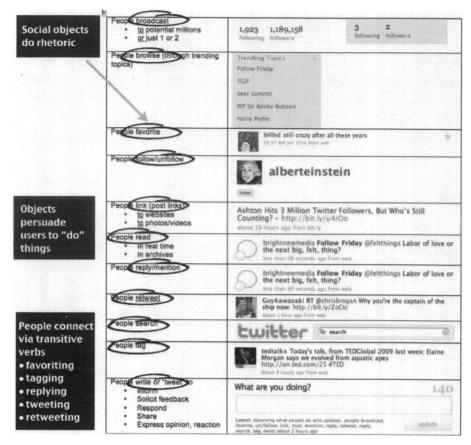

Figure 4.3. Mapping object-oriented practices on Twitter

Knowledge Cultures

The Uniform Project was a powerful example of how a social object can ignite a community and ultimately create a general knowledge culture "in which specific knowledge cultures are embedded" (Cetina, 2007, p. 369). As outlined by The Uniform Project (n.d.-a), Sheena Matheiken set out in May 2009 to wear one dress for 365 days to raise money for the Akanksha Foundation. That year, as The Uniform Project also noted, the project became a global platform for sustainable designers and hand-crafters to showcase their work through clothing donations to the project. During its second year, The Uniform Project (n.d.-b) shifted gears to serve as a platform to host various pilot projects from around the world. Community members told Matheiken that they, too, wanted to wear a dress for a set amount of time to raise money for various causes. Matheiken saw this as an opportunity to grow the project and the cause.

We can understand more about knowledge cultures by looking at object-oriented practices via the interactions of The Uniform Project's users with the social object. In this case, the social object begins with the dress itself. However, there are a variety of ways that interest in the dress generated participation. This phenomenon is what Engeström (2005) called "social gravitational pull" (para. 6). The dress is the more significant social object that draws other social objects toward its center. The force of its gravitational pull keeps all the other objects in orbit. Here's a step-by-step description of how that happened:

1. First, people commented on Matheiken's daily posts about her dress. These comments were necessary for community building—they were a kind of cultural capital or social asset.
2. People asked to be involved and join Matheiken in her endeavor. There were a variety of ways they could do this. Fans of the project could buy copies of an identical dress, or they could buy the dress pattern to sew it themselves. Others got involved by sending vintage accessories to Matheiken to accessorize the dress. In the second year, people worldwide hosted similar 365-day dress projects themselves that Matheiken, in turn, featured and promoted on her website and social media platforms.
3. Finally, people donated money to the campaign.

A knowledge culture revolves around what people deem significant, meaningful, and valuable. People found a lot of value in Matheiken's project. It wasn't necessarily what Matheiken did that interested them—it was *why* she did it. It wasn't so much the dress but what the dress stood for. For different people, it meant different things. Fashionistas, educators, environmentalists, students, and sustainable designers all loved what Matheiken was doing and why she was doing it. People believed what she believed. They took her cause, and they made it their own. They, in turn, shared the cause with more people. This is an example of how a powerful knowledge culture is born.

When one group in the Beautiful Social Research Collaborative began working with Alex's Lemonade Stand Foundation, it became clear after conducting a social object analysis that their object was the lemonade stand itself. Alex's Lemonade Stand Foundation exists to help organize the raising of money to help find a cure and to help families who have been affected by this disease. The group found that the lemonade stand itself was the social object. In this case, the lemonade stand was about empowering people to help cure childhood cancer. Whether a participant was hosting a lemonade stand or simply buying a glass of lemonade, everyone could participate in the cure. The lemonade stand was the thing that people connected around. People were coming together due to a common goal: to cure childhood cancer. When we worked with Alex's Lemonade Stand, we worked to build a stronger community of practice centered around the lemonade stand, i.e., curing childhood cancer. We focused on conveying a strong social object (via an email campaign) that worked not only to connect people but also to keep people coming back to participate in the cure.

Knowledge cultures revolve around "object worlds" (Cetina, 2007, p. 371). This is because people create knowledge through object-oriented practice. By interacting with social objects, users come to know, create knowledge, make meaning, and create value together. When it comes to the object-oriented practice of social media, people talk a lot about how to build engaged communities online. They *should also* be talking about how to build robust knowledge cultures. Understanding an organization's knowledge culture is the key to writing, designing, and strategizing for the social web. Through studying successful practices, we begin to understand what works. We begin to understand how an audience creates a knowledge culture through its object-oriented practices via the social web. Such an understanding can help bridge an essential gap between (a) the more formal and technical aspects of design and (b) the social and cultural aspects of how objects engage users and build communities.

Drawing from Cetina (1997, 2001, 2007) and Engeström (2005), we can look at how people connect through shared objects. Students can discuss their partner's social object and the performative verbs that relate to it. How does the audience create a knowledge culture through its object-oriented practices via the partner's platforms?

Organization Storytelling Analysis

At the Beautiful Social Research Collaborative, one of the most frequent requests we receive from communities is a collaboration in "telling their story." What does it mean for an organization to tell its story? In *The Shape of Design*, Frank Chimero (2012) acknowledged that

> narrative is such a fundamental way of thinking that there are even theories that say that stories are how we construct reality for ourselves. We use them to describe who we are, what we believe, where we are going, and where we came from. (Chapter 7, para. 2)

A story, for a nonprofit, is a way for an organization (a nonhuman entity) to *humanize* itself. By leading with a heartfelt story, the organization can elicit a strong sense of *pathos or feeling* while engaging deeply with its audience personally. In our work, we encounter both "capital S" Stories and "small s" stories. If the organization's *Story* is not in place, we have observed that the organization will have an uphill battle with its content and engagement strategies. If the Story is set, the organization's content seems to work from a method of alignment and seems to fall into place more easily. Thinking through the "capital S" Story is some of the most crucial work an organization can do. When we work with an organization on storytelling, our previous media analysis work with that organization, specifically the research we conduct to find the organization's golden circle and the organization's social object, should point to the partner's capital "S" Story.

Having a conversation with the community partner about its mission, its "why," or its social objects might be exactly what that partner needs to take the organization to the next level, especially if it is a new nonprofit. This was the case in the examples of Life After Life and Young and Involved Philadelphia. Once the overarching story is determined internally, the question becomes how to communicate that story externally. Usually, this involves sharing the story on the organization's website or social media site in a narrative format through text, image, audio, or video. This larger story is one that everyone at the organization knows; it becomes part of its culture. For example, Big Brothers Big Sisters of America (n.d.) tells a compelling story of how the organization originated. In 1904, Ernest Coulter was a court clerk in New York City who was shocked when he saw the number of young boys who came through the courtroom for sentencing. Coulter thought that if these children had adult role models in their lives, they would be less likely to get into trouble with the law. By sharing this story on its website, the organization creates a personal connection to the audience and shows how one person can make a lasting difference in a child's life, as Ernest Coulter did.

Stories = Change

Many organizations want to collaborate on projects that focus on smaller stories that they share on social media platforms each day—not necessarily their larger, overarching Story. For these smaller stories, we still employ research on the golden circle and social objects, but we also include work on organizational storytelling, inspired in part by Joe Lambert, founder of StoryCenter, an organization in Berkeley, California, that runs public workshops on storytelling. Lambert (2013) has defined storytelling as a moment of change. This means that a story, any story, is about a time when *change* happened. As Lambert (2018) argued, "As you become clear about the meaning of your story, you can bring your story to life by taking us into that moment of change" (p. 59). Perhaps it is a pivotal change. Maybe it is a new perspective or insight:

> Was there a moment when things changed? Were you aware of it at the time? If not, what was the moment you became aware that things had changed? Is there more than one possible moment to choose from? If so, do they have different meanings? Which most accurately conveys the meaning in your story? Can you describe the moment in detail? (Lambert, 2018, p. 59)

According to Lambert (2013), in his digital storytelling workshops he asks participants to construct and share stories in an immersive way to take the audience to that moment of change, and he has noted that, "compelling storytellers construct scenes to show how change happened, how they dealt with it, what they were like before the change, and what they are like after" (p. 60). He has shared with readers a model of narrative storytelling that taps into metaphors for the human experience, including cycles of growth and transformation. Lambert (2013) also claimed that "addressing certain kinds of stories as part of the passage through life's stages is the oldest of narrative practices" (p. 11). Lambert (2018) argued that by being told in a way that invites empathy and reflection of shared experience, "the right story can inspire someone to get up and act, to change their position, to get others involved in a cause" (p. 143).

In *Storytelling in the Digital Age: A Guide for Nonprofits,* Campbell (2017) claimed, "Nonprofits should be using their stories to motivate the reader or the viewer to do something" (p. 72). By sharing heartfelt stories, partner organizations can inspire a call-to-action—as Campbell (2017) has put it, "the action you want a person to take after being emotionally triggered by a story" (p. 72). Calls to-action are clear and direct requests for the audience to take action, such as signing up for a newsletter, listening to a podcast, donating to a cause, signing up to attend an event, double-tapping, commenting on a post, tagging someone, or clicking the link in the profile. Campbell (2017) argued that "nonprofits should always be viewing their communications through the eyes of the donors" (p. 74). She suggested making the audience the "hero" of each smaller story or post and speaking directly to the audience, as illustrated in this example: "Because of your support, we were able to provide one hundred meals to homeless veterans this winter" (Campbell, 2017, p. 74).

Many nonprofit and community-based organizations that we work with, however, do not always feel comfortable asking for money through social media posts. Getting to know the partner organization and its values is key to building solid relationships—and this entails not constantly pushing a so-called "best practices" agenda if it doesn't suit the partner. For example, in Ellen Cushman's (2013) work "Wampum, Sequoyan, and Story: Decolonizing the Digital Archive," Indigenous stories are viewed as "epistemological centers of knowledge making" (p. 128). Cushman (2013) examined how the Cherokee stories within the digital archive invite both the storyteller and the listener to "create and hold on to the legacy of knowledge as placed and located beings who, through a series of storytelling practices, honor their experience with and in the lived experience of the Cherokees" (p. 129). Listeners of the stories are asked to "pick up, hold on to, teach others, and pass along what they are told" (Cushman, 2013, p. 129). Obviously, this is a very different kind of audience call-to-action than the one described by Campbell (2017), driven by reciprocity. We must be attuned to our partner's value systems and meaning-making practices. Our goal in organizational storytelling is to tell stories on our partner's terms.

Story Generators

Nonprofit consultant Vanessa Lockshin (2016) has acknowledged that telling stories consistently can be a formidable challenge for nonprofits, and she has suggested that busy organizations can "foster collaboration to make storytelling easier" (p. 96). Lockshin has suggested that when working with nonprofits, it can be helpful to create custom-made story collection forms using software from Google Forms or Typeform, which are widely-available tools, and that these forms can be used to collect a variety of stories from various stakeholders. The partner can then share the stories in newsletters, social media, and on the organization's website. In a November 2020 workshop called Organizational Story Mining, Lambert argued that organizations should have a "story gathering, production, and distribution mechanism to highlight the lives, accomplishments, and unique contributions of members of your team, your audience, your clients, and your stakeholders." He promoted a question-driven story collection tool. Lambert's tool asks four general questions (that can be further tailored to the organization), with an emphasis on the moment of change:

1. Tell us about your background in the subject/experience? Or conversely, why did you choose to talk about this experience?
2. What has been your unique relationship to the subject? How has it affected your life/life experiences?
3. Share an experience you had with the subject. Conversely, take us back to the moments/scenes of the experience. How has it changed you?
4. If someone new were to ask you to sum up what makes you interested or passionate about the subject/or sharing this experience, what would you say were the main lessons you have to share?

At the Beautiful Social Research Collaborative, our storytelling generation mechanism includes weekly takeovers organized by student groups. Groups create content out of first-hand accounts of everyday occurrences both in and out of the classroom because these are relatable and believable stories. We try to take stock of what is happening around us. We try to show the real story, even if it is messy or complicated. Over the years, we have developed a story generator. Our story generator is a valuable heuristic that showcases multiple ways to tell stories. Most stories can be told in more than one way. The story generator helps to determine the best way to tell the story at hand. It can be used to create a variety of content—from long-form articles, to blog posts, to social media campaigns, to takeovers, to single social media posts. Each genre of storytelling listed here that can result from our story generator is illustrated with an example:

1. **Exposé**—An investigative piece that presents facts that may surprise or shock the audience. The writer incorporates compelling facts, statistics, anecdotes, or quotes to tell a true story. An example: "What Katie Didn't Know"
2. **Historical**—A piece that tells the story of a person, place, or thing in the past. The writer usually tells readers something substantial they didn't already know in an exciting fashion. An example: "The Core of Discovery"

3. **How to**—A piece that provides guidelines for tangible or intangible actions. The writer often orders actions sequentially in a step-by-step fashion. An example: "For Many Reasons: Blood and Chocolate Pudding"

4. **Informative**—A piece that provides logical information on a specific subject. This kind of piece provides information for information's sake. The writer employs expository writing, anecdotes, facts, or figures to inform readers about a subject. Writers should cover the basics—who, what, when, where, and why. An example: "Can Social Media Save Lives?"

5. **Interview**—A piece that often appears in Q & A format, but not always. The content may have breadth or depth, but usually not both. The writer may also edit the questions and narrate the interviewee's answers. An example: "Rashida"

6. **Inspirational**—A "feel good" story. The focus of the piece is the inspirational point that the writer wants to make. An example: "Charity: Water— What We Learned in India"

7. **Personal experience/Reminiscence**—A human interest piece that features an engaging story many people can relate to or would want to read. An example: "Connecting Appalachia to the World Beyond"

8. **Personal/Professional opinion**—A piece that shares a personal or professional point of view on a subject of consequence to many people. An example: "My 10 Years of Blogging"

9. **Photo story**—A piece that uses a graphic approach to storytelling. Such a piece uses a lead photo that hooks the reader and sets the tone for the visual story. The writer may supply additional text or captions. An example: "Gift of Life"

10. **Profile**—A piece that offers a prose sketch focusing on one or more aspects of someone's personality or life. The writer may interview others who can offer insights (children, spouse, neighbors, colleagues); the writer uses each interview as a time and place of reference. An example: "The Butcher Chef"

11. **Review**—A piece sharing insights into a book, film, gadget, service, or program. The writer describes their experience in either an objective, subjective, positive, or negative light. An example: "The Social Singularity"

12. **Roundup**—A piece that serves as a collection of information tied together by one theme. Writers may organize the piece around numbers or lists. An example: "10 Uncommon Superfoods from the World of Ultra-Endurance"

To support our community partners in telling engaging stories (their larger story as well as smaller related stories), students write a summary of the organization's current storytelling strategy using the following prompts:

- What is the organization's Story?
- Where is the Story told (blog, social media, newsletter, website, etc.)?
- How is the Story told?

- Does the Story align with the organization's "why"?
- Does the Story have a moment of change? Describe this.
- Could the moment of change be expanded upon? How so?
- Does the Story invite the audience to consider issues?
- Is the Story honest, authentic, and in the first person?
- What media does the organization use to tell smaller stories (video, images, text, audio)?
- How is the audience invited to participate?

Community Partner Report

The community partner report offers our partners new approaches to engaging their audiences via emerging media. At the end of the semester, students revise and edit their media analyses and combine all that is useful into one report to present to their community partner at a meeting or event (Figure 4.4 shows students sharing a community partner report in a meeting with Foi et Joie Haiti).

The report will include a variety of sections depending on which media analyses are included. Descriptions of the possible sections follow.

Figure 4.4. Sharing a community partner report

Summary of Overall Web and Social Media Presence

This section is usually 200–400 words long and includes images, data visualizations, and screenshots. It uses background research to discuss how the community partner is rhetorically using its website; its blog; and its Twitter, Facebook, YouTube, and Instagram accounts to connect with its audience. The goal of this section is to help the partner see the current state of affairs, such as its use of platforms, the number of posts per platform, the number of followers on each platform, the number of accounts being followed by each platform, audience engagement averages, typical days and times of posts, and other relevant metrics. The report should not provide critiques or suggestions, just facts with no judgment.

Comparative Media Analysis (Mentor Accounts)

This section is typically 200–800 words long and includes images, data visualizations, and screenshots. It asks: What are the top three mentor accounts that provide the most useful examples for the community partner? How were the mentor accounts determined (for example, through word-of-mouth, case studies, hashtag searches, knowledge of direct competitors, media influencers, or number of followers)? This section contains the following sub-sections:

- **Strategy**—Students discuss each mentor account. They should consider the following questions: How are the accounts demonstrating innovation, engagement, or the phenomenon of interest? What are the accounts doing? How are they doing it?

- **Effectiveness**—Students should consider the following: Why are the mentor accounts effective? What is the evidence? In their responses, students should demonstrate an argument or cite sources from the course readings or elsewhere to back up claims.

- **Summary**—In this section, students consider how the partner could benefit from or borrow some of these ideas, strategies, and practices for this project. They should be as specific as possible when referring to the mentor accounts.

Golden Circle Analysis

This section ranges from 200–400 words long and includes images, data visualizations, and screenshots. In this section, students should connect the partner's mission statement to its golden circle—its why, how, and what. Students should describe the organization's why, how, and what from the perspective of the community partner. They should also include a graphic illustration of the partner's golden circle.

Social Object Analysis

This section is 200–400 words long and includes images, data visualizations, and screenshots. Drawing from contemporary social theorists, we can look at how people connect through shared objects. The argument here is that the object is the thing that links people together. Students should discuss the community partner's social object/s and the performative verbs that relate to it. They should consider this question: How can the organization create a knowledge culture through the use of social objects?

Organizational Storytelling Strategy

This section should be 200–800 words long and include images, data visualizations, and screenshots. To support our community partners in telling better stories (their larger Story and smaller stories), students should develop a summary of the partner's current or proposed storytelling strategy. In creating this summary, the students should rely on the organization's responses to the story generator question prompts used in the organizational storytelling strategy assignment, which focus on the organization's "moment of change."

Conclusions & Suggestions

This section is normally 400–1000 words long and includes images, data visualizations, and screenshots. In this section, students aim to answer the following questions: Based on the overall analysis, what suggestions do you have for the community partner moving forward? How can the partner employ the comparative media analysis, golden circle analysis, social object analysis, and organization storytelling analysis to connect deeply with its audience about its mission? Students should be specific in their suggestions. They should also adhere to the following recommendations for writing reports and memos: "If you are making a recommendation, say, 1) what needs to be done, 2) who should do it, 3) when and where it should be done, 4) why it should be done, 5) how it should be done" (Garner, 2012, p. 129). Students should provide a concrete example for each suggestion they make.

Works Cited or References

Students should cite all work in either APA or MLA style. They should use parenthetical citations in the text as needed.

A Few Words on Tone

The tone of the report should be knowledgeable and engaging. Bryan A. Garner (2012) has suggested writing in a professional yet relaxed manner "as if speaking directly to the recipient of your document" (p. 99). In these reports, students should always try to remain objective, neutral, or positive in their tone, rather than judgmental. Here's an example:

- Judgment: This dish tastes awful.
- Objective: This dish tastes salty.

Finding the right tone in the report is essential and will determine how the information comes across to the partner. Table 4.1 provides some favored expressions to use in reports.

Table 4.1. Terms to Frame Language in Reports

Terms we avoid	Terms we favor
Client	Community partner
Help	Collaborate, Co-research
Assist	Support
Work for	Work with, Co-create
Problems	Opportunities

For example, if we want to suggest that the organization implement a new Twitter strategy, we would not say, "Organization XYZ has a better handle on their Twitter than you do. You should probably check it out and take some notes." Instead, we could ask, "Have you considered adding more images (or asking questions in your tweets) to promote audience engagement? We have seen success when other organizations implement those practices. Here are a few examples of other organizations similar to yours that have had success with this tactic." As seen in this example, the tone of the report should be supportive and engaging rather than negative or condescending. By intentionally framing their language in this way, students become active participants in creating a culture of community-building.

Chapter 5. How Might Writing Programs Become Vital Resources to Communities?

To practice the central arguments of this book—that is, the importance of putting our community partner's gains first and how that changes our approaches to community-engaged writing—I have saved my discussion of student learning until the end. As a committed educator working at a Jesuit institution that requires rigorous ethical teaching and critical reflection, it has been a significant challenge to postpone this discussion. I suspect other writing teachers may find it just as challenging as well. This is, after all, the point. Our work and approaches to that work look different when we prioritize community partnerships.

Since 2010, I have formally and informally researched the program-level learning experiences and outcomes of the Beautiful Social Research Collaborative, the community writing program at my institution. Each year, based on teaching, peer, and partner evaluations as well as personal "field notes," I frame inquiry around student learning to ask questions such as the following:

- How can emerging communication technologies in the classroom be harnessed to embrace the public work of composition?
- How can those who teach and learn with emerging communication technologies design projects that extend beyond traditional curricular boundaries to become agents of social change?
- How might evaluation and assessment of such work cultivate a network of reciprocity within our local communities?

The questions that frame each chapter of this book arose out of the slow, informal, methodological inquiry of a particular community writing program, the Beautiful Social Research Collaborative, in its local context. I describe that inquiry in this chapter.

Study Description

While student, peer, and partner evaluations help shape the program and help assess outcomes at the program level, I wanted deeper insight into whether the desired learning outcomes were achieved at the individual level—I particularly wanted to know whether students' attitudes and beliefs changed due to working with community partners. Research indicates that "community-based methods emphasize civic and social responsibility while enacting principles of collective action such as dialogue, reflection, and advocacy as means for improving and contributing to public life" (Jones et al., 2016, p. 7). To delve deeper into student learning, I asked this research question: Does working with community writing partnerships influence "agency"—students' ideas about their ability to act in and on the world in ways that relate to civic purposes?

To address this research question about agency, I opted for a pre-test/post-test model using surveys designed to provide qualitative feedback. The pre/post-test model provides a straightforward tool to systematically gather data about student learning—specifically to gain "better feedback about whether the intervention is working in the way you expected" (Clipperton et al., 2020, p. 2). Since the pre-test and post-test survey was completed as part of routine classroom activities, it was deemed exempt by the IRB board at my institution. It should be noted that a significant limitation of the pre-test/post-test design is that it cannot detect other possible causes of results. There was also no control group for comparison. At both the beginning and the end of the semester, I asked students to reflect on their attitudes and beliefs regarding civic agency, defined as ideas about one's ability to act in and on the world in ways that relate to civic purposes. The survey prompts consisted of open-ended questions:

- Are you prepared to participate in civic life (i.e., the public life of the citizen concerned with the affairs of a community)?
- Do you feel that you have the ability to influence an organization or work with your community partner to create lasting change?
- What fosters your beliefs about your ability or inability to influence an organization or create change?
- Will your experience working with community partners this semester motivate subsequent engagement, action, or behavior in your community or your life?

Findings

Analysis of the pre-test/post-test scores indicated that more than 80% of students felt their experience and learning in the course greatly influenced their attitudes and beliefs about their capacity to create change. Students indicated they learned how to take writing and emerging media beyond the personal, beyond entertainment, and into places for activism and social change by writing with and for organizations. Students worked side-by-side with community leaders who were fighting injustices, advancing the rights of marginalized populations, and amplifying underrepresented voices, and they indicated they learned skills to harness the power of writing and rhetoric for social change through working on projects alongside these community partners. Importantly, students noted that they gained new attitudes and perspectives while working with communities committed to making change.

The study findings on agency say much about what it means to take the lead to make positive change via emerging communication technologies. Taking the lead means different things to different people. For some, it means learning how to become a social entrepreneur or an activist. For others, it means building skills in digital rhetoric (or researching how people communicate through digital discourse). For others, it means learning by doing—becoming active citizens who are empowered to act. The findings of this study fall into four main themes: design, community, power, and beliefs.

Design

Community partnerships changed the way students considered design as both a practice and an outcome. One student, Ariana M., reflected,

> I had initially assumed that people would instantaneously feel connected to a nonprofit because of their cause and the good work they do in the community—but it's really more than that. I learned that we weren't just promoting the cause—we were promoting the benefit of that cause to their multiple stakeholders.

Effective design strategically communicates the message with the community partner's core values and audience at heart. Through the community design process, students indicated they were able to understand how design can be a tool to fight systemic oppression and to work toward more equitable futures. Placed in the role of designers and design researchers, students noted they could see that what they created fostered specific values. They indicated they learned that design can be a vehicle for ethical action and transformative change.

Practically speaking, collaborating with community-based organizations is a way for students to gain real-world experience for their work with emerging media. As composition scholar Eva Brumberger (2013) noted, "For too many students, design experience is slim, and a community-based project may be their only opportunity for professional development in a given semester" (p. 114). Students can use community-based projects as opportunities to add work to their portfolios and add experience to their resumes. On a deeper level, students are also engaged in a design process that emphasizes equity and justice. As noted by the Creative Reaction Lab (2018), "Every design has an impact on equity, including the decisions we make in a community project, the blueprints created for a new building, and the policies implemented in our workplaces" (p. 11). Writing with communities helps students understand how design impacts others. Costanza-Chock (2020) has acknowledged that design processes are often "structured in ways that make it impossible to see, engage with, account for, or attempt to remedy the unequal distribution of benefits and burdens that they reproduce" (Introduction section). However, equity-based methods as used by students participating in the Beautiful Social Research Collaborative are able to ground student learning in complex intersectional considerations of gender, race, and class.

Attitudes and Beliefs

Students' attitudes and beliefs changed dramatically. Lauren K. indicated that

> collaborating with Life After Life challenged the perception I
> had of the justice system in our country being one that fights
> for fairness and equality, and it made me realize that it's actually
> one that is built on putting some people first and others last: that
> it's a system that favors the color of your skin, that it's a system
> that needs to be changed.

Significantly, students reported that working with community partners changed what they "believed was possible." Students did not feel as "completely overwhelmed" by the complexity of social issues but began to believe that they (just one caring person within a community) could take action and make positive social change.

Importantly, students can gain new attitudes and perspectives while working with communities committed to making change. According to Shah (2020), "Direct engagement can offer opportunities for college students to find meaning in their academic work and learn from community members' stories, interpretations, and feedback" (p. 45). My study indicates community writing partnerships help students develop the knowledge, skills, and attitudes necessary to promote a culture of change-making.

Community

Community-engaged teaching and learning changed the way students thought about citizenship and their role in the community. As student Anna S. indicated,

> The trajectory of my future has changed after working with
> the community farmer's market. I have always wanted to make
> things, but now I know who I really want to make things with.
> What I want to do and also where I want to work has changed
> because of this course. I want to be with an organization that
> works towards improving a community through healthy eating.

Many students indicated the experience gave them a clearer idea of how they "want to live life" and how their skills could "make a positive impact on the world."

In general, contemporary students place a high value on 21st-century literacies—collective action, collective problem solving, and democratic processes that are distributed and shared by all. Not only does the model of community-university partnerships used by the Beautiful Social Research Collaborative build 21st-century literacy skills, it creates citizen-leaders with a social conscience. A writing program's commitment to community-building and civic action offers students opportunities to address immediate real-world issues. Other researchers' findings suggest that once students are involved with social purposes and issues larger than themselves, a civic ethic is fostered, which "can allow students to link their own self-interests with public concerns" (Eble & Gaillet, 2004, p. 351). For students, working closely with organizations with purpose-driven missions leads to a greater sense of participation, activism, and desire to pursue nonprofit or community-based work after college.

Power

Working alongside community partners changed the way students thought about power. As student Maggie T. reflected,

> This semester with Internews, we learned how South Sudan does not have many news outlets that provide reputable information due to the lack of technology access in the area. This kind of barrier creates misinformation for communities, especially during a global pandemic when access to trustworthy information is necessary. This experience has led me to be more thoughtful about my privilege and how I can work with marginalized and under-resourced communities through my own work.

In addition to acknowledging the knowledge, skills, and beliefs developed in class, students reported feeling empowered to keep addressing social issues after classes have ended.

Not only do students involved in community writing projects share power and decision-making with community partners, but they also see their work influence decision-making, mission statements, and policies at nonprofits and local organizations. Seeing that their work has value leads to more empowerment, capacity-building, and leadership development. Not only does the experience prepare students for the real world, but also it seems to "prepare students for changing the world" (Prell, 2003, p. 187).

Conclusion

How might writing programs become vital resources to communities? How do we see our research as a form of community building? What does it look like to center community building in our work? This book charts a path for engaging in a process that intentionally builds community through writing programs. There are many pathways to center community building in our work and our programs, each specific to local contexts and communities and each requiring more than just a shift in mindset. If we are committed to a process that builds community, it will require a continued reimagining of our approaches to program building—particularly our approaches to equity, our investment in intentional infrastructure, and our commitment to decolonial methods.

Equity-Based Approaches

As argued in the field's literature, community-engaged projects have histori-cally benefitted the university at the expense of the community. As Jennifer Bay (2019) described, "Drive-by service-learning projects, un-usable or missing end products, publications that are not shared with community partners, and failed partnerships are plentiful in the literature on service-learning and community engagement" (p. 10). When we shift the focus to putting the community first and viewing our partnerships as a community-building enterprise, we can better com-mit to creating conditions for reciprocity and mutuality with our partners. An equity-based approach demands that we commit to a process that helps us con-sider how power, oppression, resistance, privilege, penalties, benefits, and harms are systematically designed into the very systems we want to change. A commit-ment to "equity requires us to redesign structures and processes to consciously redistribute power across role groups and institutions. Co-creation acknowledges that we build **with** and not **for** others—we invite, engage and design solutions and co-produce knowledge in partnership" (National Equity Project, n.d., We Believe section). Equity-based approaches to community writing, as detailed in Chapter 2, offer a flexible method for conducting with communities design research that can point us toward more just and equitable partnerships.

Infrastructural Approaches

In light of our history of inequitable partnerships, approaches to infrastructure need to be intentionally addressed. As discussed in Chapter 1, community-en-gaged initiatives and programs are frequently "sporadic, disconnected or redun-dant, supported by individual faculty, specific funding or fleeting leadership, without incentives for broad-based support or long-term institutional commit-ment" (Yates & Accardi, 2019, p. 6). When designing infrastructural approaches to community writing projects, not only do we need to consider how to share power and knowledge with our partners, we need to support the building of internal capacity from within our local communities. As John P. Kretzman and John L. McKnight (1993) argued, "Outside resources will largely be wasted if the internal capacity of the community is not developed" (p. 376). In our work with community partners in inner-city Philadelphia, we have seen grassroots initiatives create resources from within—rather than rely on outside resources and assistance. For example, the West Philly Tool Library lends tools (donated by the community) to community members for home maintenance, repairs, and DIY projects, much as a book lending library operates. Another organi-zation, Prevention Point, which began syringe services in North Philadelphia in 1991, now serves the community in various ways, including the provision of overdose prevention education, the distribution of naloxone, and the provision of housing, meals, and legal services. Instead of imposing new partnerships and programs on communities, we can ask how "existing centralized institutions can support local invention rather than act as the inventor" (Kretzman & McKnight, 1993, p. 372). We can imagine programs that are defined by their "capacity to respond to community," rather than manage, replicate and proliferate local initiatives" (Kretzman & McKnight, 1993, p. 372). Our efforts to build capacity from within communities will highlight those communities' "ability to shape their worlds through relational and collaborative tools and solutions (Escobar, 2018, p. 20).

Decolonial Approaches

Without a commitment to decolonial approaches in our partnerships, we risk the danger of contributing to the reproduction of systemic oppression. A focus on design that encompasses the impact (and the unintentional impact) behind an outcome creates pathways for us to consider the potential consequences of design and to recognize that we have significant accountability within the partnership. Even as we work to dismantle oppressive forces, we will still falter—such as when we put our agendas before the community's agenda, when we serve the status quo, and when we make unquestioned assumptions. Engaging in opportunities for continuous reflection and improvement, for humility, for recognizing where we may cause harm and where we made the wrong choices ultimately allows for a process of change and transformation to occur. Community writing needs approaches that will not privilege imperialist or university agendas; that will not further cause harm, oppress, or victimize our community partners; that will not privilege or rely on expert knowledge; and that will not attempt to control and codify knowledge and meaning making practices in the name of progress. Writing partnerships can leverage community-building approaches to support local grassroots activism, decolonization efforts, co-resistance movements, and social change initiatives. By centering solidarity in our work, design can be "an ethical praxis of world-making" (Escobar, 2018, p. 313).

Community-building work is vital work. brown (2017) proposed that

> we can align our behavior, our structure and our movements with our visions of justice and liberation, and give those of us co-creating the future more options for working with each other and embodying the things we fight for—dignity, collective power, level generative conflict, and community. (p. 6)

The simple and straightforward question—*Are we engaging in a process that builds community?* —supports us as we work to honor and uphold the knowledges, dignity, strengths, and resources of our communities. Supporting community-led visions and grassroots organizing in our communities is the path toward transformative change. As the Highlander Research and Education Center (n.d.-a) has affirmed,

> Together, we will continue to spark radical imagination in our work to manifest another world that we know is possible, where our communities are transformed and our people are liberated. The building of that world is underway, but its foundation will not and cannot rest atop the roots of white supremacy. (para. 5)

The approaches illustrated in this book support us in doing that work—that is, the work of moving away from colonized educational systems that privatize, abstract, and codify knowledge and toward more grassroots, collaborative, and place-based approaches to building bridges of understanding and support with our local communities.

References

Allied Media Conference. (n.d.) *Track or network gathering FAQ!* Retrieved January 10, 2022, from https://amc.alliedmedia.org/amc2022-faq-for-proposing-a-track -or-network-gathering.

Allied Media Projects. (n.d.) *Network principles.* Retrieved January 10, 2022, from https://alliedmedia.org/network-principles.

And Also Too (n.d.). Retrieved January 10, 2022, from *Who participates? Who is impacted? Who benefits?* https://www.andalsotoo.net/.

Anzaldúa, G. (1981). La Prieta. In C. Moraga & G. Anzaldúa (Eds.), *This bridge called my back: Writings by radical women of color* (1st ed., pp. 198–209). Persephone Press.

Anzaldúa, G. (1987). *Borderlands / La Frontera: The New Mestiza.* Aunt Lute Books.

Ball, K. & Goodburn, A. M. (2000). Composition Studies and Service Learning: Appealing to Communities? *Composition Studies, 28*(1), 79–94. https://digitalcom mons.unl.edu/englishfacpubs/15/.

Barker, D. (2004). The scholarship of engagement: A taxonomy of five emerging practices. *Journal of Higher Education Outreach and Engagement, 9*(2), 123–137. https://openjournals.libs.uga.edu/jheoe/article/view/890/889.

Barnhart, B. (2020, September 22) How to conduct a speedy social media audit *Sprout Social.* https://sproutsocial.com/insights/social-media-audit/.

Bay, J. (2019). Research justice as reciprocity: Homegrown research methodologies. *Community Literacy Journal, 14*(1), 7–25. https://doi.org/10.25148/CLJ.14.1.009053.

Benjamin, R. (2019). *Race after technology: Abolitionist tools for the new Jim code.* Polity.

Bennett, S. & Maton, K. (2010). Beyond the "digital natives" debate: Towards a more nuanced understanding of students' technology experiences. *Journal of Computer Assisted Learning, 26*(5), 321–331. https://doi.org/10.1111/j.1365-2729.2010.00360.x.

Bennett, W. L. (Ed.). (2008). *Civic Life Online: Learning How Digital Media Can Engage Youth.* MIT Press.

Berila, B. (2015). *Integrating mindfulness into anti-oppression pedagogy: Social justice in higher education.* Routledge. https://doi.org/10.4324/9781315721033.

Bernardo, S. & Monberg, T. G. (2019). Resituating reciprocity within longer lega- cies of colonization: A conversation. *Community Literacy Journal, 14*(1), 83–93. https://doi.org/10.25148/CLJ.14.1.009058.

Big Brothers Big Sisters of America. (n.d.) *History that spans more than a century.* Retrieved January 10, 2022, from https://www.bbbs.org/history/.

BlackSpace. (n.d.). *BlackSpace manifesto.* Retrieved January 10, 2022, from https:// www.blackspace.org/manifesto.

Blouin, D. D. & Perry, E. M. (2009). Whom does service learning really serve? Com- munity-based organizations' perspectives on service learning. *Teaching Sociology, 37*(2), 120–135. https://doi.org/10.1177/0092055X0903700201.

Bojar, K. (2016). *Green shoots of democracy in the Philadelphia Democratic Party.* She Writes Press.

Bortolin, K. (2011). Serving ourselves: How the discourse on community engagement privileges the university over the community. *Michigan Journal of Community Service Learning*, *18*(1), 49–58. http://hdl.handle.net/2027/spo.3239521.0018.104.

Boston University Center for Antiracist Research. (n.d.). Be antiracist. Retrieved January 10, 2022, from https://www.bu.edu/antiracism-center/.

Boyer, E. L. (1996). The scholarship of engagement. *Journal of Public Service and Outreach*, *1*(1), 11–20. https://openjournals.libs.uga.edu/jheoe/article/view/666/666.

Boyle-Baise, M. & Efiom, P. (1999). *The construction of meaning: Learning from service learning* (ED429923). ERIC. http://files.eric.ed.gov/fulltext/ED429923.pdf.

brown, a. m. (2017). *Emergent strategy: Shaping change, shaping worlds*. AK Press.

Brown, T. (2009). *Change by design: How design thinking transforms organizations and inspires innovation*. Harper Business.

Brumberger, E. (2013). Teaching visual communication through community-engaged projects. In E. R. Brumberger & K. M. Northcut (Eds.), *Designing texts: Teaching visual communication* (pp. 99–116). Baywood Publishing Company.

Buchanan, R. (1992). Wicked Problems in Design Thinking. *Design Issues*, *8*(2), 5–21. https://doi.org/10.2307/1511637.

Burkett, I. (2012). *An introduction to co-design*. Ingrid Burkett Social Innovation. http://ingridburkett.com/wp-content/uploads/2017/09/Introduction-to-Codesign-2.pdf.

Campbell, J. (2017). *Storytelling in the digital age: A guide for nonprofits*. Charity-Channel Press.

Campus Compact. (n.d.-a). *Equity based service learning*. Retrieved April 26, 2021, from https://compact.org/resource-posts/equity-based-service-learning/.

Campus Compact. (n.d.-b) *The Ernest A. Lynton Award for the Scholarship of Engagement*. Retrieved November 28, 2021, from https://compact.org/impact-awards/ernest-a-lynton-award/.

Campus Compact. (n.d.-c). *Who we are*. Retrieved January 10, 2022, from https://compact.org/who-we-are/.

The Center for Digital Humanities at Princeton. (n.d.) *JUST Data Lab*. Retrieved January 10, 2022, from https://cdh.princeton.edu/engage/undergraduates/just-data-lab/.

Cetina, K. K. (1997). Sociality with objects: Social relations in postsocial knowledge societies. *Theory, Culture & Society*, *14*(4), 1–30. https://doi.org/10.1177/026327697014004001.

Cetina, K. K. (2001) Objectual practice. In T. R. Schatzki, K. K., Cetina & E. von Savigny (Eds.), *The practice turn in contemporary theory* (pp. 175–188). Routledge.

Cetina, K. K. (2007). Culture in global knowledge societies: Knowledge cultures and epistemic cultures. *Interdisciplinary Science Reviews*, *32*(4), 361–375. https://doi.org/10.1179/030801807X163571.

Checkoway, B. (2015). Research as community-building: Perspectives on the scholarship of engagement. *Gateways: International Journal of Community Research and Engagement*, *8*(1), 139–149. https://doi.org/10.5130/ijcre.v8i1.4240.

Chimero, F. (2012). *The shape of design*. https://shapeofdesignbook.com/.

Clipperton, J., Franco, J., Nordyke, S., Shaffer-O'Connell, M. & Wood, F. (2020). *SOTL research design for assessment of interventions*. APSA Preprints. https://doi.org/10.33774/apsa-2020-gwflo.

Collins, P. H. (1990). *Black feminist thought: Knowledge, consciousness, and the politics of empowerment*. Unwin Hyman.

Commission on Public Purpose in Higher Education. (n.d.) *Community engagement classification (U.S.)*. Retrieved January 7, 2022. https://public-purpose.org/initiatives/carnegie-elective-classifications/community-engagement-classification-u-s/.

Conference on College Composition and Communication. (2016, April). *CCCC Statement on Community-Engaged Projects in Rhetoric and Composition*. https://cccc.ncte.org/cccc/resources/positions/community-engaged.

Cooks, L. & Scharrer, E. (2006). Assessing learning in community service learning: A social approach. *Michigan Journal of Community Service Learning, 13*(1), 44–55. http://hdl.handle.net/2027/spo.3239521.0013.104.

Costanza-Chock, S. (2014). *Out of the shadows, into the streets! Transmedia organizing and the immigrant rights movement*. MIT Press. https://doi.org/10.7551/mitpress/9780262028202.001.0001.

Costanza-Chock, S. (2018). Design justice: Towards an intersectional feminist framework for design theory and practice. In C. Storni, K. Leahy, M. McMahon, P. Lloyd & E. Bohemia (Eds.), *Design as a catalyst for change—DRS International Conference 2018*. DRS Digital Library. https://doi.org/10.21606/drs.2018.679.

Costanza-Chock, S. (2020). *Design justice*. MIT Press. https://design-justice.pubpub.org/.

Crabtree, R. D. (2008). Theoretical foundations for international service-learning. *Michigan Journal of Community Service Learning, 15*(1), 18–36. http://hdl.handle.net/2027/spo.3239521.0015.102.

Creative Reaction Lab. (n.d.). *Mobilizing tomorrow's leaders to design racial and health equity—today!* Retrieved January 10, 2022, from https://www.creativereactionlab.com.

Creative Reaction Lab. (2018). *Field guide: Equity-centered community design* [Booklet]. https://www.surveymonkey.com/r/ECCDfieldguidedownload.

Creative Reaction Lab. (2019, September 23). Redesigners for justice: The leaders we need for an equitable future. *Medium*. https://medium.com/equal-space/redesigners-for-justice-the-leaders-we-need-for-an-equitable-future-d3a73459ba60.

Cross, N. (1982). Designerly ways of knowing. *Design Studies, 3*(4), 221–227. https://doi.org/10.1016/0142-694X(82)90040-0.

Cross, N. (2011). *Design Thinking: Understanding How Designers Think and Work*. Berg.

Cruz, N. I. & Giles, D. E., Jr. (2000). Where's the community in service-learning research? *Michigan Journal of Community Service Learning, Special*(1), 28–34. http://hdl.handle.net/2027/spo.3239521.spec.104.

Cushman, E. (1996). The rhetorician as an agent of social change. *College Composition and Communication, 47*(1), 7–28. https://doi.org/10.2307/358271.

Cushman, E. (2013). Wampum, Sequoyan, and Story: Decolonizing the digital archive. *College English, 76*(2), 115–135. https://library.ncte.org/journals/ce/issues/v76-2/24269.

Dadurka, D. & Pigg, S. (2011). Mapping complex terrains: Bridging social media and community literacies. *Community Literacy Journal*, *6*(1), Article 3.

Danley, S. & Christiansen, G. (2019). Conflicting responsibilities: The multidimensional ethics of university/community partnerships. *Journal of Community Engagement and Scholarship*, *11*(2), Article 3. https://digitalcommons.northgeor gia.edu/jces/vol11/iss2/3.

d'Arlach, L., Sánchez, B. & Feuer, R. (2009). Voices from the community: A case for reciprocity in service-learning. *Michigan Journal of Community Service Learning*, *16*(1), 5–16. http://hdl.handle.net/2027/spo.3239521.0016.101.

Davis, K. L., Kliewer, B. W. & Nicolaides, A. (2017). Power and reciprocity in partnerships: Deliberative civic engagement and transformative learning in community-engaged scholarship. *Journal of Higher Education Outreach and Engagement*, *21*(1), 30–54. https://openjournals.libs.uga.edu/jheoe/article/view/1316.

Deans, T. (2010). "English Studies and Public Service" in Deans, T., Roswell, B. S. & Wurr, A. J. *Writing and Community Engagement: A Critical Sourcebook* (pp. 97–116). Bedford/St. Martin's.

Design Justice Network. (n.d.). *Design justice network principles.* Retrieved January 10, 2022, from https://designjustice.org/read-the-principles.

Design Justice Network. (2016, May 2). Generating shared principles. *Design Justice Network News*. https://designjustice.org/news-1/2016/05/02/2016-generating -shared-principles.

Diehl, A., Grabill, J. T., Hart-Davidson, W. & Iyer, V. (2008). Grassroots: Supporting the knowledge work of everyday life. *Technical Communication Quarterly*, *17*(4), 413–434. https://doi.org/10.1080/10572250802324937.

Doberneck, D. M., Glass, C. R. & Schweitzer, J. (2010). From rhetoric to reality: A typology of publically engaged scholarship. *Journal of Higher Education Outreach and Engagement*, *14*(4), 5–35. https://openjournals.libs.uga.edu/index.php/jheoe /article/view/794.

Dostilio, L. D., Brackmann, S. M., Edwards, K. E., Harrison, B., Kliewer, B. W. & Clayton, P. H. (2012). Reciprocity: Saying what we mean and meaning what we say. *Michigan Journal of Community Service Learning*, *19*(1), 17–32. http://hdl .handle.net/2027/spo.3239521.0019.102.

Driscoll, A. (2008). Carnegie's community-engagement classification: Intentions and insights. *Change: The Magazine of Higher Learning*, *40*(1), 38–41. https://doi.org /10.3200/CHNG.40.1.38-41.

Eble, M. F. & Gaillet, L. L. (2004). Educating "community intellectuals": Rhetoric, moral philosophy, and civic engagement. *Technical Communication Quarterly*, *13*(3), 341–354. https://doi.org/10.1207/s15427625tcq1303_7.

Engeström, J. (2005, April 13). Why some social network services work and others don't—or: The case for object-centered sociality. *Zengestrom*. https://www.zen gestrom.com/blog/2005/04/why-some-social-network-services-work-and -others-dont-or-the-case-for-object-centered-sociality.html.

Equity Design Collaborative. (n.d.) *We crafted these definitions to create shared language as we go about building the field.* Retrieved January 10, 2022, from https:// www.equitydesigncollaborative.com/language.

Erickson, T. (2012, April 5). The biggest mistake you (probably) make with teams. *Harvard Business Review*. https://hbr.org/2012/04/the-biggest-mistake-you -probab.

Escobar, A. (2018). *Designs for the pluriverse: Radical interdependence, autonomy, and the making of worlds*. Duke University Press.

Fitzgerald, H. E., Bruns, K., Sonka, S. T., Furco, A. & Swanson, L. (2012). The centrality of engagement in higher education. *Journal of Higher Education Outreach and Engagement*, 16(3), 7–28. https://openjournals.libs.uga.edu/jheoe/article/view /949.

Fitzgerald, H. E., Smith, P., Book, P. & Rodin, K. (2005). *CIC Reports: Resource guide and recommendations for defining and benchmarking engagement DRAFT*. Committee on Institutional Cooperation. https://www.academia.edu/40668805/Re source_Guide_and_Recommendations_for_Defining_and_Benchmarking_ Engagement_DRAFT.

Flower, L. (2008). *Community literacy and the rhetoric of public engagement*. Southern Illinois University Press.

García, R. & Baca, D. (2019) Introduction: Hopes and visions: The possibility of decolonial options. In R. García & D. Baca (Eds.), *Rhetorics elsewhere and otherwise: Contested modernities, decolonial visions* (pp. 1–48). Conference on College Composition and Communication/National Council of Teachers of English.

Garner, B. A. (2012). *HBR guide to better business writing*. Harvard Business Review Press.

Grabill, J. T. (2007). *Writing community change: Designing technologies for citizen action*. Hampton Press.

Grabill, J. (2010). Infrastructure outreach and the engaged writing program. In S. K. Rose & I. Weiser (Eds.), *Going public: What writing programs learn from engagement* (pp. 15–28). Utah State University Press. https://doi.org/10.2307/j.ctt4cg pfh.4.

Grain, K. M. & Lund, D. E. (2016). The *social justice turn*: Cultivating "critical hope" in an age of despair. *Michigan Journal of Community Service Learning*, 23(1), 45–59. https://doi.org/10.3998/mjcsloa.3239521.0023.104.

Gram, M. (2019). On design thinking. *N+1*. (35). https://nplusonemag.com/issue-35 /reviews/on-design-thinking/.

Granovetter, M. S. (1973). The strength of weak ties. *American Journal of Sociology*, 78(6), 1360–1380. https://doi.org/10.1016/B978-0-12-442450-0.50025-0.

Greenwood, D. J. (2008). Theoretical research, applied research, and action research: The deinstitutionalization of activist research. In C. R. Hale (Ed.), *Engaging contradictions: Theory, politics, and methods of activist scholarship* (pp. 319–340). University of California Press. https://doi.org/10.1525/9780520916173-016.

Gunatillake, R. (2017). *Modern mindfulness: How to be more relaxed, focused, and kind while living in a fast, digital, always-on world*. St. Martin's Griffin.

Haas, A. M. (2012). Race, rhetoric, and technology: A case study of decolonial technical communication theory, methodology, and pedagogy. *Journal of Business and Technical Communication*, 26(3), 277–310. https://doi.org/10.1177/105065 1912439539.

Hanh, T. N. (2008). *The art of power.* HarperOne.

Harrison, R., Blickem, C., Lamb, J., Kirk, S. & Vassilev, I. (2019). Asset-based community development: Narratives, practice, and conditions of possibility—a qualitative study with community practitioners. *SAGE Open, 9*(1). https://doi.org /10.1177/2158244018823081.

Hartman, E. (2015). A strategy for community-driven service-learning and community engagement: Fair trade learning. *Michigan Journal of Community Service Learning, 22*(1), 97–100. http://hdl.handle.net/2027/spo.3239521.0022.113.

Highlander Research and Education Center. (n.d.-a). *Justice would be George Floyd still being here.* Retrieved January 10, 2022, from https://myemail.constant contact.com/-The-state-can-t-give-us-transformative-justice——Mariame-Kaba. html?soid=1114995572350&aid=z49xv3eunqg.

Highlander Research and Education Center. (n.d.-b). *Mission and methodologies.* Retrieved January 10, 2022, from https://highlandercenter.org/our-story/mission/.

Holland, B. A. (2005) Reflections on community-campus partnerships: What has been learned? What are the next challenges? In P. A. Pasque, R. E. Smerek, B. Dwyer, N. Bowman & B. L. Mallory (Eds.), *Higher education collaboratives for community engagement and improvement* (pp. 10–17) (ED515231). ERIC. http:// files.eric.ed.gov/fulltext/ED515231.pdf.

Hyphen-Labs. (n.d.). *About us.* Retrieved January 10, 2022, from http://www.hyphen -labs.com/about.html.

Jameson, J. K., Clayton, P. H. & Jaeger, A. J. (2011). Community engaged scholarship through mutually transformative partnerships. In L. M. Harter, J. Hamel-Lambert & J. Millesen (Eds.), *Participatory partnerships for social action and research* (pp. 259–277). Kendall Hunt.

Janke, E. (2018). Increased community presence is not a proxy for reciprocity. *EJournal of Public Affairs, 2*(2), 1–23. https://www.ejournalofpublicaffairs. org/2-2-1-increased-community-presence-is-not-a-proxy-for-reciprocity/.

Jen, N. (2017, August 11). Natasha Jen: Design thinking is bullsh*t [Video transcript]. 99U. https://99u.adobe.com/videos/55967/natasha-jen-design-thinking-is-bullshit.

Jenkins, H., Shresthova, S., Gamber-Thompson, L., Kligler-Vilenchik, N. & Zimmermann, A. M. (2016). *By any media necessary: The new youth activism.* New York University Press. https://opensquare.nyupress.org/books/9781479829712 /read/.

Jones, N. N. (2016). The technical communicator as advocate: Integrating a social justice approach in technical communication. *Journal of Technical Writing and Communication, 46*(3), 342–361. https://doi.org/10.1177/0047281616639472.

Jones, N. N. (2020). Coalitional learning in the contact zones: Inclusion and narrative inquiry in technical communication and composition studies. *College English, 82*(5), 515–526. https://library.ncte.org/journals/ce/issues/v82-5/30756.

Jones, N. N., Moore, K. R. & Walton, R. (2016). Disrupting the past to disrupt the future: An antenarrative of technical communication. *Technical Communication Quarterly, 25*(4), 211–229. https://doi.org/10.1080/10572252.2016.1224655.

Kimbell, L. (2011). Rethinking design thinking: Part I. *Design and Culture, 3*(3), 285–306. https://doi.org/10.2752/175470811X13071166525216.

Kincaid, J. (1978, June 19). Girl. *The New Yorker.* https://www.newyorker.com /magazine/1978/06/26/girl.

Kissane, R. J. & Gingerich, J. (2004). Do you see what I see? Nonprofit and resident perceptions of urban neighborhood problems. *Nonprofit and Voluntary Sector Quarterly, 33*(2), 311–333. https://doi.org/10.1177/0899764004263519.

Kohl-Arenas, E., Alston, K. & Preston, C. (2020) *Leading and learning initiative: Shifting institutional culture to fortify public scholarship.* Imagining America. https://imaginingamerica.org/wp-content/uploads/IA_Network_report_December_2020.pdf.

Kolbert, E. (2017, February 19). Why facts don't change our minds. *The New Yorker.* https://www.newyorker.com/magazine/2017/02/27/why-facts-dont-change-our -minds.

Kretzmann, J. P. & McKnight, J. L. (1993). *Building communities from the inside out: A path toward finding and mobilizing a community's assets.* ACTA Publications. https://resources.depaul.edu/abcd-institute/publications/Pages/basic-manual.aspx.

Lambert, J. (2013). *Seven stages: Story and the human experience.* Digital Diner Press.

Lambert, J. (with Hessler, B.). (2018). *Digital storytelling: Capturing lives, creating community* (5th ed.). Routledge. https://doi.org/10.4324/9781351266369.

Langley, J., Wolstenholme, D. & Cooke, J. (2018). 'Collective making' as knowledge mobilisation: The contribution of participatory design in the co-creation of knowledge in healthcare. *BMC Health Services Research, 18*(1), Article 585. https:// doi.org/10.1186/s12913-018-3397-y.

Lawson, B. (1980). *How designers think.* Architectural Press.

Leverenz, C. S. (2014). Design thinking and the wicked problem of teaching writing. *Computers and Composition, 33,* 1–12. https://doi.org/10.1016/j.compcom.2014.07.001.

Lewin, K. (1946). Action research and minority problems. *Journal of Social Issues,* 2(4), 34–46. https://doi.org/10.1111/j.1540-4560.1946.tb02295.x

Life After Life. (n.d.). About. Retrieved January 10, 2022, from https://lifeafterlife. home.blog/about/.

Lockshin, V. C. (2016). *The storytelling nonprofit: A practical guide to telling stories that raise money and awareness.* Lockshin Consulting.

Lockwood, T. (Ed.). (2010). *Design thinking: Integrating innovation, customer experience and brand value.* Allworth Press.

Lohr, J. & Lindenman, H. (2018). Challenging audiences to listen: The performance of self-disclosure in community writing projects. *Community Literacy Journal, 13*(1), 71–86. https://doi.org/10.25148/CLJ.13.1.009091.

Mac, T. (2020, June 9). Compassionate action over empathy. *Bah-hum-blog.* https:// tatianamac.com/posts/mistakes.

Mansfield, H. (2012). *Social media for social good: A how-to guide for nonprofits.* McGraw-Hill.

Manzini, E. (2015). *Design, when everybody designs: An introduction to design for social innovation* (R. Coad, Trans.). MIT Press.

Marback, R. (2009). Embracing Wicked Problems: The Turn to Design in Composition Studies. *College Composition and Communication, 61*(2), 397–419. https:// library.ncte.org/journals/CCC/issues/v61-2/9494.

Mathieu, P. (2005). *Tactics of hope: The public turn in English composition.* Boynton/Cook.

Mathieu, P. (2014). Excavating indoor voices: Inner rhetoric and the mindful writing teacher. *JAC, 34*(1/2), 173–190.

McKercher, K. A. (2020). *Beyond sticky notes: Co-design for real: Mindsets, methods and movements.* Beyond Sticky Notes.

McKim, R. (1972). *Experiences in visual thinking.* Brooks/Cole.

Mignolo, W. D. (2007). Delinking: The rhetoric of modernity, the logic of coloniality and the grammar of de-coloniality. *Cultural Studies, 21*(2–3), 449–514. https://doi.org/10.1080/09502380601162647.

Miller, M. (2017, February 16). Want to fight inequality? Forget design thinking. *Fast Company.* https://www.fastcompany.com/3068235/want-to-fight-inequality-forget-design-thinking.

Mission Investors Exchange. (2019, January). *Racial equity: Foundational concepts.* https://missioninvestors.org/resources/racial-equity-foundational-concepts.

Mitchell, T. D., Donahue, D. M. & Young-Law, C. (2012). Service learning as a pedagogy of whiteness. *Equity & Excellence in Education, 45*(4), 612–629. https://doi.org/10.1080/10665684.2012.715534.

National Equity Project. (n.d.). *Creating a world that works for all of us.* Retrieved January 10, 2022, from https://www.nationalequityproject.org/.

Nelson, C. L. (1991). The National SEED Project. *Educational Leadership, 49*(4), 66–67. https://www.ascd.org/el/articles/the-national-seed-project.

Patel, L. (2015). *Decolonizing educational research: From ownership to answerability.* Routledge. https://doi.org/10.4324/9781315658551.

Pearl, D. (2020). Learning is not the destination. *Journal of Community Engagement and Scholarship, 13*(1), Article 2. https://digitalcommons.northgeorgia.edu/jces/vol13/iss1/2/.

Phillips, A. A. L. (2018, January 25). *"Thoughts from a formerly condemned man-child": Aaron "Abd'Allah Lateef" Phillips reflects on Miller and Montgomery rulings.* Juvenile Law Center. https://medium.com/@JuvLaw1975/thoughts-from-a-formerly-condemned-man-child-aaron-abdallah-lateef-phillips-reflects-on-eocffcdbe74f.

Plastrik, P., Taylor, M. & Cleveland, J. (2014). *Connecting to change the world: Harnessing the power of networks for social impact.* Island Press.

Powell, K. M. & Takayoshi, P. (2003). Accepting roles created for us: The ethics of reciprocity. *College Composition and Communication, 54*(3), 394–422. https://doi.org/10.2307/3594171.

Prell, C. L. (2003). Web writing and service learning: A call for training as a final deliverable. In J. A. Inman, C. Reed & P. Sands (Eds.), *Electronic collaboration in the humanities: Issues and options.* Routledge.

Purdy, J. P. (2014). What can design thinking offer writing studies? *College Composition and Communication, 65*(4), 612–641.

Rander, M. & Wellers, D. (n.d.). Digital social objects: The emotional glue of customer experiences. *SAP Insights.* Retrieved January 10, 2022, from https://insights.sap.com/digital-social-objects-the-emotional-glue-of-customer-experiences/.

Reichelt, L. (2007, March 1). Ambient intimacy. *Disambiguity*. https://www.disambi guity.com/ambient-intimacy/.

Reid, D. R. (2015, September 15). Over the rainbow—Why *Looking for Charlie* is black and white. *Race and Resistance in American Popular Culture and Cinema*. http://www.darrenreidhistory.co.uk/over-the-rainbow-why-looking-for-charlie -is-black-and-white/.

Research Action Design. (n.d.). *About us*. Retrieved January 10, 2022, from https:// rad.cat/about/.

Rheingold, H. (2007). Using participatory media and public voice to encourage civic engagement. In W. Lance Bennett (Ed.), *Civic life online: Learning how digital media can engage youth* (pp. 97–118). MIT Press. https://doi.org/10.7551/ mitpress/7893.003.0006.

Rittel, H. W. J. & Webber, M. M. (1973). Dilemmas in a general theory of planning. *Policy Sciences, 4*(2), 155–169. https://doi.org/10.1007/BF01405730.

Rosenstein, J. & De Carlo, K. (n.d.). How to define your team's mission. *Wavelength*. Retrieved January 10, 2022, from https://wavelength.asana.com/how-define -your-company-mission-statement/.

Saltmarsh, J. A. & Hartley, M. (2012). Introduction. In J.A. Saltmarsh & M. Hartley (Eds.), *"To serve a larger purpose": Engagement for democracy and the transformation of higher education*. Temple University Press.

Saltmarsh, J., Hartley, M. & Clayton, P. (2009). *Democratic engagement white paper* [White paper]. New England Resource Center for Higher Education. https:// scholarworks.umb.edu/nerche_pubs/45/.

Sanders, B.-N. (2002). From user-centered to participatory design approaches. In J. Frascara (Ed.), *Design and the Social Sciences* (pp. 1–8). CRC Press.

Sandy, M. & Holland, B. A. (2006). Different worlds and common ground: Community partner perspectives on campus-community partnerships. *Michigan Journal of Community Service Learning, 13*(1), 30–43. http://hdl.handle.net/2027/spo .3239521.0013.103.

Schatzki, T. R. (2001). Introduction. In T. T. Schatzki, K. K. Cetina & E. von Savigny (Eds.), *The practice turn in contemporary theory*. Routledge.

Shah, R. W. (2020). *Rewriting partnerships: Community perspectives on community-based learning*. Utah State University Press.

Shah, R. W., Selting Troester, J. M., Brooke, R., Gatti, L., Thomas, S L. & Masterson, J. (2018). Fostering eABCD: Asset-based community development in digital service-learning. *Journal of Higher Education Outreach and Engagement, 22*(2), 189–222. https://openjournals.libs.uga.edu/jheoe/article/view/1391.

Shih, C. (2011). *The Facebook era: Tapping online social networks to market, sell, and innovate* (2nd ed.). Prentice Hall.

Shumake, J. & Shah, R. W. (2017). Reciprocity and power dynamics: Community members grading students. *Reflections: A Journal of Community-Engaged Writing and Rhetoric, 17*(2), 5–42. https://reflectionsjournal.net/2019/10/reciprocity-and -power-dynamics-community-members-grading-students-by-jessica-shumake -rachael-wendler-shah/.

Simon, H. (1981). *The sciences of the artificial* (2nd ed.). MIT Press.

Sinek, S. (2011). *Start with why: How great leaders inspire everyone to take action.* Portfolio/Penguin.

Sinek, S. (2017). *Find your why: A practical guide to discovering purpose for you or your team.* Portfolio/Penguin.

Spelic, S. (2018, January 14). What if? And what's wrong? Design thinking and thinking about design we can't easily see. *Medium.* https://edifiedlistener.med ium.com/what-if-and-whats-wrong-f617ada90216.

Stratos Innovation Group. (2016, October 15). Co-design: A powerful force for creativity and collaboration. *Medium.* https://medium.com/@thestratosgroup/co -design-a-powerful-force-for-creativity-and-collaboration-bed1e0f13d46.

Taggart, A. R. (2007). One or many? Tensions with authorship and evaluation in community engagement writing. *Michigan Journal of Community Service Learning, 13*(2), 53–65. http://hdl.handle.net/2027/spo.3239521.0013.205.

Taufen, A. (2018). Dear prudence: Power, campus-community collaborations, and the elusive space between constructive disruption and neoliberal subcontract. *Conflux, 12,* 1–20. https://digitalcommons.tacoma.uw.edu/conflux/12/.

Twitter. (n.d.). *Twitter for good: Using the positive power of Twitter to strengthen our communities.* Retrieved January 10, 2022, from https://about.twitter.com/en /who-we-are/twitter-for-good.html.

The Elective Classification for Community engagement. Carnegie Elective Classifications. (2022, January 26). Retrieved January 29, 2022, from https://carnegieelec tiveclassifications.org/the-elective-classification-for-community-engagement-2/.

The Uniform Project. (n.d.-a). *Year 1—How it all began.* Retrieved January 10, 2022, from https://theuniformproject.com/our-story/.

The Uniform Project. (n.d.-b). *Year 2—30 day pilots.* Retrieved January 10, 2022, from https://theuniformproject.com/30-day-pilots/.

Vernon, A. & Ward, K. (1999). Campus and community partnerships: Assessing impacts and strengthening connections. *Michigan Journal of Community Service Learning, 6*(1), 30–37. http://hdl.handle.net/2027/spo.3239521.0006.103.

Vinsel, L. (2017, December 6). Design thinking is kind of like syphilis—It's contagious and rots your brains. *Medium.* https://sts-news.medium.com/design-think ing-is-kind-of-like-syphilis-its-contagious-and-rots-your-brains-842ed078af29.

Walton, R. W., Moore, K. R. & Jones, N. N. (2019). *Technical communication after the social justice turn: Building coalitions for action* (1st ed.). Routledge.

Weingarten Learning Resources Center. (2017, January 9). Writing strategies: What's your positionality? *The Weingarten Blog.* https://weingartenlrc.wordpress.com /2017/01/09/research-writing-whats-your-positionality/.

Wessels, B. (2018). *Communicative civic-ness: Social media and political culture* (1st ed.). Routledge. https://doi.org/10.4324/9781315660653.

Wible, S. (2020). Using design thinking to teach creative problem solving in writing courses. *College Composition and Communication, 71*(3), 399–425. https://library .ncte.org/journals/CCC/issues/v71-3/30501.

Yates, J. J. & Accardi, M. (2019). *Field guide for urban university-community partnerships.* University of Virginia Institute for Advanced Studies in Culture. http:// iasculture.org/research/publications/thriving-cities-field-guide.

Zamenopoulos, T. & Alexiou, K. (2018). *Co-design as collaborative research*. Connected Communities Foundation Series. Bristol University; AHRC Connected Communities Programme. http://oro.open.ac.uk/58301/.

Zavala, M. (2016). Decolonial methodologies in education. In M. A. Peters (Ed.), *Encyclopedia of Educational Philosophy and Theory* (Living ed.). Springer. https://doi.org/10.1007/978-981-287-532-7_498-1.

Appendices

Appendix A. Positionality Activity

Providing an opportunity to interrogate how race, class, and gender shape identity can be a good starting place for community work. Students and teachers will undoubtedly confront socialized and entrenched notions of privilege, identity, and social justice within the context of this work. Learning more about *positionality* is a step toward this process of inquiry. This includes looking at how we are *positioned* (by ourselves, by others, by particular discourse communities) in relation to multiple relational social processes of difference (gender, class, race, ethnicity, age, sexuality). Doing this work means looking at how we are each differently positioned in hierarchies of power and privilege.

In my teaching, I employ a tactic similar to what Cathy L. Nelson (1991) described as occurring at a National SEED (Seeking Educational Equity and Diversity) Project on Inclusive Curriculum seminar. According to Nelson, during the seminar, participants interrogated positionality by writing short stories reminiscent of the Jamaica Kincaid story "Girl." She recalled,

> During our first moments together as a community of scholars/
> learners, we read aloud personal versions of Jamaica Kincaid's
> "Girl," drawing upon the gendered and remembered voices
> from our own pasts. The first voices we heard were our own.
> Immediately, we recognized the authenticity and power of our
> own lived experience. (Nelson, 1991, p. 66).

I use the same strategy to create a more open and inclusive tone in the classroom. Reflecting on positionality by sharing our own versions of "Girl" opens an exciting learning process. Not only does this activity help students learn ways to start theorizing subjectivity, it helps set the tone for sharing our experiences in the classroom. Jamaica Kincaid's (1978) "Girl" voices a character's experience growing up in the West Indies, with the story beginning as follows:

> Wash the white clothes on Monday and put them on the stone
> heap; wash the color clothes on Tuesday and put them on the
> clothesline to dry; don't walk bare-head in the hot sun; cook
> pumpkin fritters in very hot sweet oil.

We can consider the story as an interior monologue—a stream of thoughts or emotions running through the character's mind. To begin the lesson, the class may read or listen to the short story together. I have my students read along while listening to Kincaid narrate her story aloud (available at https://www.youtube .com/watch?v=AHr1HYWomKE).

Discussion

Next, students participate in a discussion. In small groups or in a larger class discussion, they examine the following questions:

- What is the significance of the story's title?
- How has the character internalized messages about how one "should" act?
- Which statements in the story are based on judgments, assumptions, beliefs, opinions, values, and concepts in the character's mind?
- Which statements are non-judgmental—describing reality as it is, factual data, without added value judgments of "good" and "bad"/"should" or "shouldn't"?
- Which judgments are treated as facts in the story?
- Which judgments does the character internalize?

It's worth taking time here to note that Mathieu (2014) referred to the form of monologue represented by "Girl" as interior rhetoric—"stories we tell ourselves about ourselves, our tacit beliefs about how the world works or doesn't" (p. 180). This means we should consider that judgments in stories like this are thoughts based on opinion; they are not statements of universal fact based in reality. Mathieu (2014) wrote that "excavating one's inner rhetoric is an ongoing process, which begins by becoming mindful of one's thoughts and labeling them as thoughts" (p. 182). "Inner rhetoric is powerful," Mathieu (2014) claimed, "not because it is true, but because we act and behave as if it is true" (p. 184.) The following writing activity enables us to initiate our own inquiry in order to observe our "inner rhetoric" as an instance of *internalized oppression*—the idea that we need to understand how oppression works more clearly in ourselves before seeing how it works in communities. We do this to deepen our capacities to bear witness to each other's lived experiences and work together to build more compassionate and just communities.

Community scholar Beth Berila (2015) noted that "internalized oppression often takes the form of a brutal inner voice that does not speak our inner wisdom but instead reinforces the harmful narratives of the dominant culture" (p. 68). This means that believing our thoughts can be a kind of unconscious self-sabotage. Berila (2015) also noted that "power systems have infiltrated our psyches to such an extent that we conform without necessarily realizing we are doing so and without recognizing the deeply damaging effects that conformity has on our own way of being" (p. 68). Sometimes we may find internalized oppression manifesting itself in the things we thought we held most dear—in our very achievements and values.

Pre-writing Activity

In this pre-writing activity, students do some of the excavation work of their own inner rhetoric and oppression. They consider which judgments or "internal rhetoric" they currently hold about themselves that are masquerading as facts. In a notebook, they jot down an example for each of the following bullet points:

- When is a time something has been judged as meeting a standard or not?
- When is a time someone was judged or labeled as good or bad?
- When is a time when had a strong attachment to a value and believed you were right?
- When is a time you judged yourself?
- When is a time you judged someone else?
- Where have we internalized these messages? We may have never had the opportunity to stop and consider how these messages may or may not fit for us. How do the messages we receive both from ourselves and from others shape us?
- Do you judge your appearance when you look in the mirror?
- Do you think certain people are more attractive than others?
- Do you think certain people are more popular than others?
- Who do you resent?
- What do you lash out at?
- What do you believe is better than? "X is better than Y."
- What do you believe is worse than? "X is worse than Y."
- Where do you feel included?
- Where do you feel excluded?
- Where do you see others as separate from you?
- Where do you feel like an outsider?
- In what ways do you habitually ignore, marginalize, erase, or dismiss other (different) points of view?
- Which of the following identities have you internalized, and in what ways: national, racial, class, ability, sexual, gender, linguistic, cultural, ethnic, religious, spiritual?
- Which messages from your family, friends, communities, and society have you internalized?
- What do you believe in, and where do these beliefs come from?

When they are finished, they can take some time to share their responses.

Writing Activity

After considering the above questions, which involves taking an inventory of their value judgments and beliefs, students write their own authentic version of "Girl" in about 250–750 words. They write their stories as interior monologues, similar to Kincaid's. In them, they describe and interrogate the beliefs about the world and themselves that they have inherited and assembled along the way. They consider the following questions: Which of your stories, thoughts, assumptions, and beliefs empower you? Which of your stories, thoughts, assumptions, and beliefs limit you? Which are your own? Which are inherited? Where did they come from? Which do you have a conflict with? Which are you unsure of? Which do you want to let go of because they no longer serve you? They should draw on the remembered voices of their pasts as well as the current stories they tell themselves. This is free writing. They should use this time to answer the questions in the form of a story. No one ever has to see this draft.

Student Example

Nathan K.—"Boy"

Sort your clothes into darks and lights; wash the darks in cold water and the lights in hot; never walk in bare feet in the grass, there could be nails hiding there; always look both ways before crossing the street–twice; on time is late–always be early; it's fine to get a grade below an A, it just means you didn't do your best this time around; when you're under my roof you go to Mass every Sunday, or Saturday night if that works better for you–God sees it either way; this is how you pull weeds; this is how you rinse dishes before putting them in the dishwasher; this is how you pray–you should do that every night; this is how you suppress an emotion; this is how you avoid a fight with your spouse; you cannot have sleepovers with boys because of who you are; you cannot have sleepovers with girls because of who you are, men and women should not sleep in the same room unless they are married; this is how to be a role model to your brother; *but I've already explained why nothing bad would happen if you let me;* this is how to stick to a commitment you have made; this is how to stick to a commitment that has been made for you by somebody else; this is how to clip your nails; this is how to clip a cat's nails; this is how to clean a cat scratch so it doesn't get infected; this is how to make a bed; this is how to pay attention to your surroundings–you should leave if you feel threatened in any capacity whatsoever; this is how to be the bigger person; separate your trash from your recycling, it's our duty to protect the planet God has given us; ignore the remarks your grandmother makes, thank goodness I'm not like her; if you can, always solve a problem yourself, even if you're not properly equipped to do so; this is how to dress yourself; this is how to take care of your body; this is how to cook vegetables; this is how to cook soup; this is how to cook pasta; this is how to cook grilled cheese; this is how to cook pancakes; this is how to make cookies; this is how to sound dignified when you answer a phone; if somebody asks for money, always consider what they might use it for before giving it; this is how to make a budget; this is how to drive–do you have to go so fast?; *I'm barely going the speed limit;* this is how to water a plant; this is how to forget to water a plant; this is how to dispose of a dead plant; this is how to throw rotten apples off the deck for the squirrels; this is how to throw moldy bread off the deck for the birds; this is how to pack a suitcase; this is how to pack a school bag; this is how to read a train schedule; don't forget a toothbrush; this is how you should speak to adults; drink almond milk, it won't cause cancer like cow's milk will; don't believe everything you read on the internet; go play outside in the sun, it's good for you; this is how to decorate a Christmas tree; this is how to open one present every hour to make Christmas last all day; you are on your own path with God–someday you'll be exactly where I am; this is how to help those who are less fortunate–this will help when you're at Heaven's gates; this is how to receive Holy Communion; this is how to behave in Church; *but what if I'm just different than you are?*; this is how to sing harmony; this is how to play piano; this is how to make a wine spritzer; this is how to laugh until you can't breathe; you can tell me anything–just don't expect the answer to be exactly what you want to hear; if you're not looking for advice, you shouldn't complain; this is how to hide who you are for your sake; this is why you should hide who you are for my sake; this is how to tell somebody you love them without using your words; always send a thank you card–it's the right thing to do; use the gifts that have been given to you; you always make us proud–everybody has high expectations for you; this is how to apply for a job; this is how to plan for your future; *but what if I still don't know what I want to do, or who I want to be?*; take a deep breath. There's so much more time than you think–why do you worry so much?

Sharing and Discussion

When the writing assignment is complete, students sit in a circle, and I ask for volunteers to read their stories aloud. No students *have to* share their stories. However, I let students know that if they want to share their writing, it will be welcomed and very beneficial in making the class a safe space to work against internalized and institutionalized oppression.

After hearing some readings from the class, I ask students to contemplate some of the following questions in a large-group discussion:

- Where are the similarities in the stories?
- Where are the differences?
- How do gender, race, and power crop up?
- How does race and privilege (or the lack thereof) come into play?
- In what ways do we believe the stories we tell ourselves?
- In what ways is it helpful to believe these stories?
- In what ways is it unhelpful?
- How can we revise the voices in our heads?
- How do we dismantle the negative messages we receive?
- How can we become more accepting of reality as it is and reduce our judgmental thoughts?
- What was it like to write this story about yourself?
- What did you learn in writing it?
- We have come to this place from many different backgrounds. How do we make space for all of the complex identities that are in the room?

- How can we work so as not to alienate anyone's voice?
- How do we work so as not to invalidate anyone's experience?
- How do we frame this class as one that fosters inclusion—not just in our discussions here, but also when we work with community partners outside the classroom walls?

We discuss the ideas that the experiences we have and how we interpret these experiences shape our beliefs, attitudes, personalities, and interior rhetoric. We note that it's vital to take an honest account of the stories we tell ourselves and listen deeply to them. We acknowledge that if we find we are beating ourselves up for having any of these thoughts, we should pause and listen deeply. We consider that we should meet these "attacks" with compassion. We aim to remember that we are doing this work in the spirit of self-compassion, not self-destruction.

I let students know that this activity is an invitation to become more familiar with how internalized oppression works in ourselves before seeing how it works in communities. As mindfulness writer Rohan Gunatillake (2017) urged, "Those of us who take care of ourselves from the inside out not only make a real difference to themselves but also the world around them" (p. 223). I ask students to acknowledge (and if need be, interrogate) their beliefs in order to see things as they are. I suggest that by noting the instances where we have difficulty non-judgmentally describing the facts, we can begin to uncover underlying root causes.

Appendix B. Roles on Teams

Team members share a common goal—active involvement in a successful project. There are many moving parts to achieve that goal. The success of a community project takes everyone working together—researching, writing, editing, designing, and presenting. Some shared responsibilities of team members include

- participating actively in in-class and out-of-class meetings,
- completing readings between class meetings,
- completing assignments between class meetings,
- participating in multiple off-campus visits with the community partner,
- completing all projects according to the determined schedule, and
- completing reflections and evaluations.

These are the responsibilities of all team members. In addition to assigning these general responsibilities, issuing specifically designed roles for team members gives each person on the team a sense of ownership; each person becomes invested in the project's outcome, thereby increasing the likelihood of a better overall plan. Tammy Erickson (2012) explained that

> collaboration improves when the roles of individual team members are clearly defined and well understood—in fact, when individuals feel their role is bounded in ways that allow them to do

a significant portion of their work independently. Without such clarity, team members are likely to waste energy negotiating roles or protect turf rather than focus on the task. The Harvard Business Review writes: "We've also found that team members are more likely to want to collaborate if the path to achieving the team's goal is left somewhat ambiguous. If a team perceives the task as one that requires creativity, where the approach is not yet well known or predefined, its members are more likely to invest more time and energy in collaboration (Erickson). (para. 3)

Without assigning specific roles, members may grow disinterested or detached and possibly territorial over parts of the project.

There are various roles that can be assigned for any given team, and the roles may vary depending on the nature of each project. One position, however, is mandatory for each group. One responsible person should be chosen as the *point of contact*. The community partner will only send and receive email messages or phone calls with this one team member. It is this team member's duty to communicate with the rest of the team in a clear and timely manner. When multiple people in the group send emails to community partners, it can be very confusing for everyone, and messages do not always meet their intended targets (for example, everyone in the group might not receive the latest partner updates and information). Just one responsible member should be chosen to be the point of contact to communicate on behalf of the team for the entirety of the semester project.

Other roles for team members are generally not as formal as the role of point of contact, but that is not to say they are less critical. One person may take on multiple roles, as well. The available roles may include the following:

- *Facilitator*—The person in this role issues meeting agendas before the meeting to allow for review, comment, and revisions to the agenda. Distributing agendas in advance of the meeting may also lead to more productive discussions as participants are more likely to be prepared.
- *Organizer*—The person holding this position communicates to stakeholders about the status and progress of stated goals.
- *Scheduler*—The scheduler keeps everyone organized through Asana, Slack, Google Calendar, or other similar software. This person is responsible for sending reminders to the rest of the group.
- *Notetaker*—This person writes and posts a detailed record of all meetings.
- *Analyst*—The person in this position regularly writes analytical memos about the team's internal processes and decisions.
- *Documentarian*—This person visually documents the work of the group through photographs and videos.
- *Content creator*—The person holding this role crafts updates for social media about the course and the community partnership.

While each team in the class is organized through the various roles held by its members, it is the instructor's responsibility to make sure the teams have what they need to ensure a successful project. The instructor's role includes

- issuing a call for community partners,
- confirming the participation of community partners before the course begins,
- facilitating class discussions and activities,
- assuring each group stays focused on its stated goals and outcomes,
- preparing groups for their community partner meetings,
- following up with each group after their community partner meetings,
- overseeing each group's community project,
- facilitating reflections, and
- facilitating final evaluations from students and community partners.

Appendix C. Locating Community Partners

When the Beautiful Social Research Collaborative is ready to accept new partners for the upcoming semester, we sometimes put out a public call through social media channels to request proposals from interested organizations. When we issue these calls, we usually do so about six weeks before the start of the next semester. We issue a call for partners via a blog post or through Twitter, Facebook, or Instagram. Generocity, a web platform for social good in Philadelphia, has featured our calls for partners to great success. Such platforms exist in many towns. Indeed.com is also an effective space to post a call for partners. In our calls, we ask potential organizations to draft a short proposal for a project via a contact form or email.

Lately, we have had more requests through the contact page on our website than we can handle, so we have not needed to issue a formal call for partners. However, we have issued formal calls for partners in the past, and the following sections contain an example call for partners, an example inquiry we received through our website, and a description of the process of selecting community partners to work with.

An Example Call for Partners

Subject: Seeking new project partners:

The new semester is almost here, and the Beautiful Social Research Collaborative is currently open to new collaborative partnerships that will run September-November. Our goal is to build capacity with local communities and organizations. We are passionate about using the web to make positive social change. If you are a nonprofit or community-based organization, we have teams of talented students who would like to partner with your organization to:

- Conduct research
- Consult on social media strategies
- Co-create web, video content, or a social media campaign
- Organize workshops, technology training, or resources

To view some of our previous projects, please follow the link to "Our Work." https://www.beautifulsocial.org/work

Send us your ideas for collaboration,

The Beautiful Social Team

An Example of an Inquiry from Our Website Contact Form

Name: Jacqueline K.

Organization: Hope Partnership for Education

Organization Website: http://www.hopepartnershipforeduca tion.org/.

Message: At Hope Partnership, our mission is to break the cycle of poverty through education in Eastern North Philadelphia by providing children and adults with individualized learning opportunities. We serve children, families, and individuals in Eastern North Philadelphia who live below the poverty level and struggle in traditional educational settings. We are hoping that Beautiful Social can help us tell our story better through video. We have our annual event coming up in October, and we would love to create a video/slideshow (about 5 minutes long) to encourage giving from donors. We would also use this video for various future needs.

Selecting Community Partners

A few weeks after we issue a call, our community partner list begins to take shape. After a follow-up phone call with the potential partner, we have a good working knowledge of what our new partners hope to achieve by working with the collaborative. It can be helpful at this stage to ask partners to discuss in more detail the specific problem or area of interest they would like to pursue in a research project well in advance of the actual project start date. We then notify our partners when they will hear from the team that will be working with them.

We generally accept four to five partners each semester. Class enrollment usually runs at 18–24 students. Our student teams are organized with four to five students per team; however, many different configurations could work. If one partner is all you have, it will still work, with student teams working on various aspects of the project.

At times, our public calls elicit more responses than we can handle. We find that the people who direct our local nonprofit organizations often wear many hats and have modest financial resources, little time, and little to no formal training when it comes to engaging and building communities online. Many are eager to pursue a research partnership. Also, our growing list of partners helps in building our "street cred" around town. When we have more valid requests than we can handle, we usually ask potential partners if they would be willing to pursue a project during another semester. We currently have a waitlist of about six months.

Everywhere I go, I seem to run into someone affiliated with a nonprofit or a worthy cause that would be a great fit for a collaborative partnership. Rather than relying on finding our partners this way, however, we rely on previous partners and social media recommendations to issue a call for community partners. That is to say, my rule of thumb for locating community partners is to let them find us. This is a general rule, learned from being a Peace Corps Volunteer, not a hard and fast one. We have reached out to organizations when I have intuited a good fit. However, we have found that sometimes when we approach an organization, that community partner can view a project through the lens that they are "helping the class" or "doing us a favor." Once this tone is established, it is hard to eradicate it. Students begin to lose some of their agency as researchers in a collaborative and are viewed instead as "just students" in a course. This dynamic can lead to less-than-optimal projects for a variety of reasons. It may be a subtle psychological shift, but it is a noticeable one.

In contrast, when community partners seek out B: Social, there is a greater likelihood that the nonprofit's level of motivation will match that of the student team members'. At the beginning of this program, we did not have this luxury of choice. I have included my reflections about both situations here for consideration.

Appendix D. Meeting With Community Partners

One of the most critical aspects of the Beautiful Social Research Collaborative process is our meetings with community partners. Students regularly meet with community partners via Zoom, face-to-face, or a combination of both. We try to have students visit the organization's office or sponsored event whenever possible. I usually do not attend these meetings. Everybody has different teaching philosophies and methods, but I would advise instructors to resist attending these meetings. Even when I sit on the sidelines, my presence at a meeting can shift the power dynamic in my direction (and I'm a relatively quiet person!). It is vital to allow students to take the lead in holding these conversations for themselves, as this is where the most growth occurs. Usually, a "senior student" or "fellow" who has taken the class before is included on each team. The senior student or fellow is there for support but is instructed not to take the lead in the meeting—this student should only facilitate as needed. The meetings with community partners are meant to provide students with real-world experience. They are opportunities for development and learning.

Travel Logistics

We make sure to work out the travel logistics ahead of time. In a large city like Philadelphia, this means that students will arrange their travel by public transportation such as bus or train, by university van (with the prerequisite training), or by their own vehicles. Students should give plenty of time for contingencies in traveling to the site, such as late trains or busses, parking issues, accidents, etc. It's a good idea to research the destination ahead of time to know exactly where students are going in advance and to determine where they will park (if driving) by using Google Maps' street view or similar technology.

Teams should plan to travel together or to meet up together on the street or parking lot before entering the building. When the entire group arrives, team members take a few deep breaths and then enter the building quietly (without chatter) and with confidence. They go directly to the front desk and introduce themselves calmly as "[name], from [university]." They make sure in advance that they know who they are meeting with and ask for that person by name. Once that person arrives, the students can introduce themselves with "[name], from [university]."

Meeting Expectations

For some students, the first meeting is understandably anxiety inducing. Even if students have held jobs or internships before this course, stepping into the role of a research consultant can be an entirely new experience. To help ease that feeling of the unknown, here are a few things students can expect when meeting with community partners:

- A professional conference-like setting: When invited to a community partner's office, we will most likely meet in an office or conference room.
- One or more people at the meeting: The liaison may not be working alone. Any number of people from the organization might be attending the sessions, including partners, assistants, directors, project managers, or interns. We try to expect the unexpected—more people than we think may show up to this meeting.
- Community partner dressed in business or business casual clothing: Many organizations uphold a business casual dress code. We maintain professionalism by adhering to business casual attire. (This could look

like dark jeans or slacks paired with a button-down shirt, blouse, or sweater, or jacket.)

Running the Meeting

Once students are situated in the meeting area, it's a good idea to start with introductions. Students introduce themselves by mentioning their majors and minors—nothing too revealing. Everyone in the room should be invited to introduce themselves, including their roles or job titles. If the partner doesn't initiate this, students should feel free to take the lead, as it is vital to know who is in the room.

Before the meetings, students often create an agenda, which someone in the group has shared with the partner via a Google Doc so that everyone can edit it. The students print extra hard copies of this plan to pass around the room. This agenda will be the roadmap for the meeting. When in the meeting, students should feel free to call on their team members by name to help the organization put names to faces. Simply stating, "Joe will now tell you about current research on Twitter strategies . . . " allows for the meeting to be more personal.

Meeting Tips

When meeting with community partners, the following tips will not only help students to make a good impression but will also help participants feel more in control:

- **Be present**—make eye contact, shake hands with everyone there.
- **Be engaged**—keep cell phones silent and away from view.
- **Be visible**—get out from behind the laptop. Designate one person from the team to take notes in a notebook or a computer (a notebook is preferred). The other team members remain engaged in the conversation and as tech-free as possible.
- **Be audible**—speak clearly; try to enunciate. Be mindful of tempo; it's easy to talk or read too quickly when nervous.
- **Be composed**—be mindful of body language. When nervous, some people tend to cover their mouths when they speak, play with their hair, fidget with things, rock or spin their chair, or laugh excessively (because, nerves!). Stay mindful and in the moment.
- **Be focused**—stay on task. If the community partner asks questions of a personal or off-topic nature, respond politely but without too much detail and then proceed with the meeting agenda.
- **Be prepared**—try not to come empty-handed. Whether it be a report, a presentation, a handout, a PowerPoint, or simply a printed plan to share, show up to the meetings prepared. The more prepared you can be, the smoother the meeting will go. Meeting agendas outline the topics

planned for discussion or the objectives planned to be achieved at the meeting. Send the schedule to stakeholders in a Google Doc about a week before the meeting to allow everyone a chance to review, comment, and revise the agenda as needed. A shared plan encourages everyone to be prepared and allows for a more productive discussion.

- **Be professional**—thank those you've met with for their time and let them know when they will hear back with the next steps.

Appendix E. Facilitating Reflection

Reflections are a way for team members to share their current state of being. I say "state of being" here, as this time serves as a counterpoint to the "states of doing" we usually invest in. Reflections are a time for students to let their guards down and step away from the need to be strategic and tactical. Students find reflections useful in processing events, as they are a place to share, vent, troubleshoot, anticipate, and ask questions. These are especially important after a meeting or event with community partners. Berila (2015) contended that "self-reflection is a process, so each time we engage in it, we have the opportunity to do deeper and become more nuanced in our understanding of ourselves and others" (p. 86). Reflections are a time to consider events from a deeper perspective so students can better understand themselves and their community partners.

I urge making the time for these checkpoints—place a high value on the process of meaningful reflection and inquiry. I ask each student to spend about 15–20 minutes writing a personal or team reflection for the week before we discuss our observations as a class. After the reflection process, we regroup as a class to voice our thoughts and share our experiences. We hear updates from each team and listen to group members who want to share their experiences or their questions. We can then begin to look deeper into what has happened during the week from a more nuanced standpoint. I guide students to move beyond their personal experience and toward an analysis of why these reactions occurred. How do our reactions and assumptions shape our perceptions? If there is a point of tension or discomfort, we ask: What am I feeling? Does this remind me of anything? Have I felt this way before? How can we address this and move forward? How can we open spaces for connection rather than division?

In the following sections, I provide some individual reflection prompts, some group reflection prompts, and a final reflection assignment.

Individual Reflection Prompts

- Here's what I expected . . .
- Here's how I thought it would go . . .
- Here's how it went . . .
- Here's what surprised me or caught me off guard . . .

- Here's what challenged me . . .
- Here's what I learned . . .
- Here's what I wish I knew beforehand . . .
- Here's what I still need to know . . .
- Here's what I anticipate for next time . . .
- Here are my current questions . . .

Group Reflection Prompts

- What worked?
- What went well?
- What are the benefits of the project?
- Did we accomplish our goals and outcomes (so far)?
- What didn't work?
- What were the issues?
- How can we move forward?
- How can we improve?
- Were there surprises?
- What surprised us or caught us off guard?
- What can we learn from these surprises?
- What would we do differently, with hindsight?
- How could we have been better prepared?
- How did we work well together?
- How did we not work so well together?
- What did we assume?
- Where were the pressure points?
- Where was the discomfort, tension, or conflict?
- Was it handled?
- How can we handle it?
- What was learned as a result of the conflict/s?
- Were we unprepared?
- What did we do right?
- Where did we mess up?
- How can we learn from this?
- What did we learn in this project (so far)?
- What did we do in this project that could transfer to other projects?
- What do we need to know or acquire for next time?
- How can we plan better next time around?
- Who is already doing this kind of work well?
- Are there creative approaches we can borrow or adapt?
- What unanswered questions do we have?
- What do we need to succeed?

Final Reflection Assignment

Gloria Anzaldúa (1981) once wrote,

> *The pull between what is and what should be.* I believe that
> by changing ourselves we change the world, that traveling El
> Mundo Zurdo path is the path of a two-way movement—a
> going deep into the self and an expanding out into the world, a
> simultaneous recreation of the self and a reconstruction of soci-
> ety. (p. 208)

How is the world (or society) transformed when the self is transformed? Anzaldúa
(1987) also wrote, "Nothing happens in the 'real' world unless it first happens in
the images in our heads" (p. 87). This final assignment asks you to write a short
350–750 word reflection that tells a story about transformation based on your
collaboration with community partners this semester. This can be about a change
that occurred professionally, ethically, civically, morally, academically, psycho-
logically, internally, intellectually, emotionally, or spiritually. Use specific details
in your account to bring the writing to life for the reader. Make sure to keep your
writing focused on your topic—now is not the time to discuss the entire semester's worth of events—just focus on telling one story of change.

Index